Projects: A Very Short Introduction

VERY SHORT INTRODUCTIONS are for anyone wanting a stimulating and accessible way into a new subject. They are written by experts, and have been translated into more than 45 different languages.

The series began in 1995, and now covers a wide variety of topics in every discipline. The VSI library now contains over 500 volumes—a Very Short Introduction to everything from Psychology and Philosophy of Science to American History and Relativity—and continues to grow in every subject area.

Very Short Introductions available now:

ACCOUNTING Christopher Nobes
ADOLESCENCE Peter K. Smith
ADVERTISING Winston Fletcher
AFRICAN AMERICAN RELIGION
    Eddie S. Glaude Jr
AFRICAN HISTORY John Parker and
    Richard Rathbone
AFRICAN RELIGIONS
    Jacob K. Olupona
AGEING Nancy A. Pachana
AGNOSTICISM Robin Le Poidevin
AGRICULTURE Paul Brassley and
    Richard Soffe
ALEXANDER THE GREAT
    Hugh Bowden
ALGEBRA Peter M. Higgins
AMERICAN HISTORY Paul S. Boyer
AMERICAN IMMIGRATION
    David A. Gerber
AMERICAN LEGAL HISTORY
    G. Edward White
AMERICAN POLITICAL HISTORY
    Donald Critchlow
AMERICAN POLITICAL PARTIES
    AND ELECTIONS L. Sandy Maisel
AMERICAN POLITICS
    Richard M. Valelly
THE AMERICAN PRESIDENCY
    Charles O. Jones
THE AMERICAN REVOLUTION
    Robert J. Allison
AMERICAN SLAVERY
    Heather Andrea Williams
THE AMERICAN WEST Stephen Aron

AMERICAN WOMEN'S HISTORY
    Susan Ware
ANAESTHESIA Aidan O'Donnell
ANARCHISM Colin Ward
ANCIENT ASSYRIA Karen Radner
ANCIENT EGYPT Ian Shaw
ANCIENT EGYPTIAN ART AND
    ARCHITECTURE Christina Riggs
ANCIENT GREECE Paul Cartledge
THE ANCIENT NEAR EAST
    Amanda H. Podany
ANCIENT PHILOSOPHY Julia Annas
ANCIENT WARFARE
    Harry Sidebottom
ANGELS David Albert Jones
ANGLICANISM Mark Chapman
THE ANGLO-SAXON AGE John Blair
ANIMAL BEHAVIOUR
    Tristram D. Wyatt
THE ANIMAL KINGDOM
    Peter Holland
ANIMAL RIGHTS David DeGrazia
THE ANTARCTIC Klaus Dodds
ANTISEMITISM Steven Beller
ANXIETY Daniel Freeman and
    Jason Freeman
THE APOCRYPHAL GOSPELS
    Paul Foster
ARCHAEOLOGY Paul Bahn
ARCHITECTURE Andrew Ballantyne
ARISTOCRACY William Doyle
ARISTOTLE Jonathan Barnes
ART HISTORY Dana Arnold
ART THEORY Cynthia Freeland

ASIAN AMERICAN HISTORY
    Madeline Y. Hsu
ASTROBIOLOGY David C. Catling
ASTROPHYSICS James Binney
ATHEISM Julian Baggini
THE ATMOSPHERE Paul I. Palmer
AUGUSTINE Henry Chadwick
AUSTRALIA Kenneth Morgan
AUTISM Uta Frith
THE AVANT GARDE David Cottington
THE AZTECS David Carrasco
BABYLONIA Trevor Bryce
BACTERIA Sebastian G. B. Amyes
BANKING John Goddard and
    John O. S. Wilson
BARTHES Jonathan Culler
THE BEATS David Sterritt
BEAUTY Roger Scruton
BEHAVIOURAL ECONOMICS
    Michelle Baddeley
BESTSELLERS John Sutherland
THE BIBLE John Riches
BIBLICAL ARCHAEOLOGY
    Eric H. Cline
BIOGRAPHY Hermione Lee
BLACK HOLES Katherine Blundell
BLOOD Chris Cooper
THE BLUES Elijah Wald
THE BODY Chris Shilling
THE BOOK OF MORMON
    Terryl Givens
BORDERS Alexander C. Diener and
    Joshua Hagen
THE BRAIN Michael O'Shea
BRANDING Robert Jones
THE BRICS Andrew F. Cooper
THE BRITISH CONSTITUTION
    Martin Loughlin
THE BRITISH EMPIRE Ashley Jackson
BRITISH POLITICS Anthony Wright
BUDDHA Michael Carrithers
BUDDHISM Damien Keown
BUDDHIST ETHICS Damien Keown
BYZANTIUM Peter Sarris
CALVINISM Jon Balserak
CANCER Nicholas James
CAPITALISM James Fulcher
CATHOLICISM Gerald O'Collins
CAUSATION Stephen Mumford and
    Rani Lill Anjum

THE CELL Terence Allen and
    Graham Cowling
THE CELTS Barry Cunliffe
CHAOS Leonard Smith
CHEMISTRY Peter Atkins
CHILD PSYCHOLOGY Usha Goswami
CHILDREN'S LITERATURE
    Kimberley Reynolds
CHINESE LITERATURE Sabina Knight
CHOICE THEORY Michael Allingham
CHRISTIAN ART Beth Williamson
CHRISTIAN ETHICS D. Stephen Long
CHRISTIANITY Linda Woodhead
CIRCADIAN RHYTHMS
    Russell Foster and Leon Kreitzman
CITIZENSHIP Richard Bellamy
CIVIL ENGINEERING David Muir Wood
CLASSICAL LITERATURE William Allan
CLASSICAL MYTHOLOGY
    Helen Morales
CLASSICS Mary Beard and
    John Henderson
CLAUSEWITZ Michael Howard
CLIMATE Mark Maslin
CLIMATE CHANGE Mark Maslin
CLINICAL PSYCHOLOGY
    Susan Llewelyn and
    Katie Aafjes-van Doorn
COGNITIVE NEUROSCIENCE
    Richard Passingham
THE COLD WAR Robert McMahon
COLONIAL AMERICA Alan Taylor
COLONIAL LATIN AMERICAN
    LITERATURE Rolena Adorno
COMBINATORICS Robin Wilson
COMEDY Matthew Bevis
COMMUNISM Leslie Holmes
COMPLEXITY John H. Holland
THE COMPUTER Darrel Ince
COMPUTER SCIENCE Subrata Dasgupta
CONFUCIANISM Daniel K. Gardner
THE CONQUISTADORS
    Matthew Restall and
    Felipe Fernández-Armesto
CONSCIENCE Paul Strohm
CONSCIOUSNESS Susan Blackmore
CONTEMPORARY ART
    Julian Stallabrass
CONTEMPORARY FICTION
    Robert Eaglestone

CONTINENTAL PHILOSOPHY
   Simon Critchley
COPERNICUS Owen Gingerich
CORAL REEFS Charles Sheppard
CORPORATE SOCIAL
   RESPONSIBILITY Jeremy Moon
CORRUPTION Leslie Holmes
COSMOLOGY Peter Coles
CRIME FICTION Richard Bradford
CRIMINAL JUSTICE Julian V. Roberts
CRITICAL THEORY
   Stephen Eric Bronner
THE CRUSADES Christopher Tyerman
CRYPTOGRAPHY Fred Piper and
   Sean Murphy
CRYSTALLOGRAPHY A. M. Glazer
THE CULTURAL REVOLUTION
   Richard Curt Kraus
DADA AND SURREALISM
   David Hopkins
DANTE Peter Hainsworth and
   David Robey
DARWIN Jonathan Howard
THE DEAD SEA SCROLLS
   Timothy H. Lim
DECOLONIZATION Dane Kennedy
DEMOCRACY Bernard Crick
DEPRESSION Jan Scott and
   Mary Jane Tacchi
DERRIDA Simon Glendinning
DESCARTES Tom Sorell
DESERTS Nick Middleton
DESIGN John Heskett
DEVELOPMENTAL BIOLOGY
   Lewis Wolpert
THE DEVIL Darren Oldridge
DIASPORA Kevin Kenny
DICTIONARIES Lynda Mugglestone
DINOSAURS David Norman
DIPLOMACY Joseph M. Siracusa
DOCUMENTARY FILM
   Patricia Aufderheide
DREAMING J. Allan Hobson
DRUGS Les Iversen
DRUIDS Barry Cunliffe
EARLY MUSIC Thomas Forrest Kelly
THE EARTH Martin Redfern
EARTH SYSTEM SCIENCE Tim Lenton
ECONOMICS Partha Dasgupta
EDUCATION Gary Thomas

EGYPTIAN MYTH Geraldine Pinch
EIGHTEENTH-CENTURY BRITAIN
   Paul Langford
THE ELEMENTS Philip Ball
EMOTION Dylan Evans
EMPIRE Stephen Howe
ENGELS Terrell Carver
ENGINEERING David Blockley
ENGLISH LITERATURE Jonathan Bate
THE ENLIGHTENMENT
   John Robertson
ENTREPRENEURSHIP Paul Westhead
   and Mike Wright
ENVIRONMENTAL ECONOMICS
   Stephen Smith
ENVIRONMENTAL LAW
   Elizabeth Fisher
ENVIRONMENTAL POLITICS
   Andrew Dobson
EPICUREANISM Catherine Wilson
EPIDEMIOLOGY Rodolfo Saracci
ETHICS Simon Blackburn
ETHNOMUSICOLOGY Timothy Rice
THE ETRUSCANS Christopher Smith
EUGENICS Philippa Levine
THE EUROPEAN UNION John Pinder
   and Simon Usherwood
EUROPEAN UNION LAW
   Anthony Arnull
EVOLUTION Brian and
   Deborah Charlesworth
EXISTENTIALISM Thomas Flynn
EXPLORATION Stewart A. Weaver
THE EYE Michael Land
FAMILY LAW Jonathan Herring
FASCISM Kevin Passmore
FASHION Rebecca Arnold
FEMINISM Margaret Walters
FILM Michael Wood
FILM MUSIC Kathryn Kalinak
THE FIRST WORLD WAR
   Michael Howard
FOLK MUSIC Mark Slobin
FOOD John Krebs
FORENSIC PSYCHOLOGY
   David Canter
FORENSIC SCIENCE Jim Fraser
FORESTS Jaboury Ghazoul
FOSSILS Keith Thomson
FOUCAULT Gary Gutting

THE FOUNDING FATHERS
R. B. Bernstein
FRACTALS Kenneth Falconer
FREE SPEECH Nigel Warburton
FREE WILL Thomas Pink
FREEMASONRY Andreas Önnerfors
FRENCH LITERATURE John D. Lyons
THE FRENCH REVOLUTION
William Doyle
FREUD Anthony Storr
FUNDAMENTALISM Malise Ruthven
FUNGI Nicholas P. Money
THE FUTURE Jennifer M. Gidley
GALAXIES John Gribbin
GALILEO Stillman Drake
GAME THEORY Ken Binmore
GANDHI Bhikhu Parekh
GENES Jonathan Slack
GENIUS Andrew Robinson
GEOGRAPHY John Matthews and
David Herbert
GEOPOLITICS Klaus Dodds
GERMAN LITERATURE Nicholas Boyle
GERMAN PHILOSOPHY
Andrew Bowie
GLOBAL CATASTROPHES Bill McGuire
GLOBAL ECONOMIC HISTORY
Robert C. Allen
GLOBALIZATION Manfred Steger
GOD John Bowker
GOETHE Ritchie Robertson
THE GOTHIC Nick Groom
GOVERNANCE Mark Bevir
GRAVITY Timothy Clifton
THE GREAT DEPRESSION AND
THE NEW DEAL Eric Rauchway
HABERMAS James Gordon Finlayson
THE HABSBURG EMPIRE Martyn Rady
HAPPINESS Daniel M. Haybron
THE HARLEM RENAISSANCE
Cheryl A. Wall
THE HEBREW BIBLE AS LITERATURE
Tod Linafelt
HEGEL Peter Singer
HEIDEGGER Michael Inwood
HEREDITY John Waller
HERMENEUTICS Jens Zimmermann
HERODOTUS Jennifer T. Roberts
HIEROGLYPHS Penelope Wilson
HINDUISM Kim Knott

HISTORY John H. Arnold
THE HISTORY OF ASTRONOMY
Michael Hoskin
THE HISTORY OF CHEMISTRY
William H. Brock
THE HISTORY OF LIFE
Michael Benton
THE HISTORY OF MATHEMATICS
Jacqueline Stedall
THE HISTORY OF MEDICINE
William Bynum
THE HISTORY OF TIME
Leofranc Holford-Strevens
HIV AND AIDS Alan Whiteside
HOBBES Richard Tuck
HOLLYWOOD Peter Decherney
HOME Michael Allen Fox
HORMONES Martin Luck
HUMAN ANATOMY Leslie Klenerman
HUMAN EVOLUTION Bernard Wood
HUMAN RIGHTS Andrew Clapham
HUMANISM Stephen Law
HUME A. J. Ayer
HUMOUR Noël Carroll
THE ICE AGE Jamie Woodward
IDEOLOGY Michael Freeden
INDIAN CINEMA
Ashish Rajadhyaksha
INDIAN PHILOSOPHY Sue Hamilton
THE INDUSTRIAL REVOLUTION
Robert C. Allen
INFECTIOUS DISEASE Marta L. Wayne
and Benjamin M. Bolker
INFINITY Ian Stewart
INFORMATION Luciano Floridi
INNOVATION Mark Dodgson and
David Gann
INTELLIGENCE Ian J. Deary
INTELLECTUAL PROPERTY
Siva Vaidhyanathan
INTERNATIONAL LAW Vaughan Lowe
INTERNATIONAL MIGRATION
Khalid Koser
INTERNATIONAL RELATIONS
Paul Wilkinson
INTERNATIONAL SECURITY
Christopher S. Browning
IRAN Ali M. Ansari
ISLAM Malise Ruthven
ISLAMIC HISTORY Adam Silverstein

ISOTOPES Rob Ellam
ITALIAN LITERATURE
    Peter Hainsworth and David Robey
JESUS Richard Bauckham
JEWISH HISTORY David N. Myers
JOURNALISM Ian Hargreaves
JUDAISM Norman Solomon
JUNG Anthony Stevens
KABBALAH Joseph Dan
KAFKA Ritchie Robertson
KANT Roger Scruton
KEYNES Robert Skidelsky
KIERKEGAARD Patrick Gardiner
KNOWLEDGE Jennifer Nagel
THE KORAN Michael Cook
LANDSCAPE ARCHITECTURE
    Ian H. Thompson
LANDSCAPES AND
    GEOMORPHOLOGY
    Andrew Goudie and Heather Viles
LANGUAGES Stephen R. Anderson
LATE ANTIQUITY Gillian Clark
LAW Raymond Wacks
THE LAWS OF THERMODYNAMICS
    Peter Atkins
LEADERSHIP Keith Grint
LEARNING Mark Haselgrove
LEIBNIZ Maria Rosa Antognazza
LIBERALISM Michael Freeden
LIGHT Ian Walmsley
LINCOLN Allen C. Guelzo
LINGUISTICS Peter Matthews
LITERARY THEORY Jonathan Culler
LOCKE John Dunn
LOGIC Graham Priest
LOVE Ronald de Sousa
MACHIAVELLI Quentin Skinner
MADNESS Andrew Scull
MAGIC Owen Davies
MAGNA CARTA Nicholas Vincent
MAGNETISM Stephen Blundell
MALTHUS Donald Winch
MAMMALS T. S. Kemp
MANAGEMENT John Hendry
MAO Delia Davin
MARINE BIOLOGY Philip V. Mladenov
THE MARQUIS DE SADE John Phillips
MARTIN LUTHER Scott H. Hendrix
MARTYRDOM Jolyon Mitchell
MARX Peter Singer

MATERIALS Christopher Hall
MATHEMATICS Timothy Gowers
THE MEANING OF LIFE
    Terry Eagleton
MEASUREMENT David Hand
MEDICAL ETHICS Tony Hope
MEDICAL LAW Charles Foster
MEDIEVAL BRITAIN John Gillingham
    and Ralph A. Griffiths
MEDIEVAL LITERATURE
    Elaine Treharne
MEDIEVAL PHILOSOPHY
    John Marenbon
MEMORY Jonathan K. Foster
METAPHYSICS Stephen Mumford
THE MEXICAN REVOLUTION
    Alan Knight
MICHAEL FARADAY
    Frank A. J. L. James
MICROBIOLOGY Nicholas P. Money
MICROECONOMICS Avinash Dixit
MICROSCOPY Terence Allen
THE MIDDLE AGES Miri Rubin
MILITARY JUSTICE Eugene R. Fidell
MILITARY STRATEGY
    Antulio J. Echevarria II
MINERALS David Vaughan
MODERN ART David Cottington
MODERN CHINA Rana Mitter
MODERN DRAMA
    Kirsten E. Shepherd-Barr
MODERN FRANCE Vanessa R. Schwartz
MODERN IRELAND Senia Pašeta
MODERN ITALY Anna Cento Bull
MODERN JAPAN
    Christopher Goto-Jones
MODERN LATIN AMERICAN
    LITERATURE
    Roberto González Echevarría
MODERN WAR Richard English
MODERNISM Christopher Butler
MOLECULAR BIOLOGY Aysha Divan
    and Janice A. Royds
MOLECULES Philip Ball
THE MONGOLS Morris Rossabi
MOONS David A. Rothery
MORMONISM Richard Lyman Bushman
MOUNTAINS Martin F. Price
MUHAMMAD Jonathan A. C. Brown
MULTICULTURALISM Ali Rattansi

MULTILINGUALISM John C. Maher
MUSIC Nicholas Cook
MYTH Robert A. Segal
THE NAPOLEONIC WARS
    Mike Rapport
NATIONALISM Steven Grosby
NAVIGATION Jim Bennett
NELSON MANDELA Elleke Boehmer
NEOLIBERALISM Manfred Steger and
    Ravi Roy
NETWORKS Guido Caldarelli and
    Michele Catanzaro
THE NEW TESTAMENT
    Luke Timothy Johnson
THE NEW TESTAMENT AS
    LITERATURE Kyle Keefer
NEWTON Robert Iliffe
NIETZSCHE Michael Tanner
NINETEENTH-CENTURY BRITAIN
    Christopher Harvie and
    H. C. G. Matthew
THE NORMAN CONQUEST
    George Garnett
NORTH AMERICAN INDIANS
    Theda Perdue and Michael D. Green
NORTHERN IRELAND
    Marc Mulholland
NOTHING Frank Close
NUCLEAR PHYSICS Frank Close
NUCLEAR POWER Maxwell Irvine
NUCLEAR WEAPONS
    Joseph M. Siracusa
NUMBERS Peter M. Higgins
NUTRITION David A. Bender
OBJECTIVITY Stephen Gaukroger
OCEANS Dorrik Stow
THE OLD TESTAMENT
    Michael D. Coogan
THE ORCHESTRA D. Kern Holoman
ORGANIC CHEMISTRY
    Graham Patrick
ORGANIZATIONS Mary Jo Hatch
PAGANISM Owen Davies
PAIN Rob Boddice
THE PALESTINIAN-ISRAELI
    CONFLICT Martin Bunton
PANDEMICS Christian W. McMillen
PARTICLE PHYSICS Frank Close
PAUL E. P. Sanders
PEACE Oliver P. Richmond

PENTECOSTALISM William K. Kay
THE PERIODIC TABLE Eric R. Scerri
PHILOSOPHY Edward Craig
PHILOSOPHY IN THE ISLAMIC
    WORLD Peter Adamson
PHILOSOPHY OF LAW
    Raymond Wacks
PHILOSOPHY OF SCIENCE
    Samir Okasha
PHOTOGRAPHY Steve Edwards
PHYSICAL CHEMISTRY Peter Atkins
PILGRIMAGE Ian Reader
PLAGUE Paul Slack
PLANETS David A. Rothery
PLANTS Timothy Walker
PLATE TECTONICS Peter Molnar
PLATO Julia Annas
POLITICAL PHILOSOPHY David Miller
POLITICS Kenneth Minogue
POPULISM Cas Mudde and
    Cristóbal Rovira Kaltwasser
POSTCOLONIALISM Robert Young
POSTMODERNISM Christopher Butler
POSTSTRUCTURALISM
    Catherine Belsey
PREHISTORY Chris Gosden
PRESOCRATIC PHILOSOPHY
    Catherine Osborne
PRIVACY Raymond Wacks
PROBABILITY John Haigh
PROGRESSIVISM Walter Nugent
PROJECTS Andrew Davies
PROTESTANTISM Mark A. Noll
PSYCHIATRY Tom Burns
PSYCHOANALYSIS Daniel Pick
PSYCHOLOGY Gillian Butler and
    Freda McManus
PSYCHOTHERAPY Tom Burns and
    Eva Burns-Lundgren
PUBLIC ADMINISTRATION
    Stella Z. Theodoulou and Ravi K. Roy
PUBLIC HEALTH Virginia Berridge
PURITANISM Francis J. Bremer
THE QUAKERS Pink Dandelion
QUANTUM THEORY
    John Polkinghorne
RACISM Ali Rattansi
RADIOACTIVITY Claudio Tuniz
RASTAFARI Ennis B. Edmonds
THE REAGAN REVOLUTION Gil Troy

REALITY Jan Westerhoff
THE REFORMATION Peter Marshall
RELATIVITY Russell Stannard
RELIGION IN AMERICA Timothy Beal
THE RENAISSANCE Jerry Brotton
RENAISSANCE ART
    Geraldine A. Johnson
REVOLUTIONS Jack A. Goldstone
RHETORIC Richard Toye
RISK Baruch Fischhoff and John Kadvany
RITUAL Barry Stephenson
RIVERS Nick Middleton
ROBOTICS Alan Winfield
ROCKS Jan Zalasiewicz
ROMAN BRITAIN Peter Salway
THE ROMAN EMPIRE
    Christopher Kelly
THE ROMAN REPUBLIC
    David M. Gwynn
ROMANTICISM Michael Ferber
ROUSSEAU Robert Wokler
RUSSELL A. C. Grayling
RUSSIAN HISTORY Geoffrey Hosking
RUSSIAN LITERATURE Catriona Kelly
THE RUSSIAN REVOLUTION
    S. A. Smith
SAVANNAS Peter A. Furley
SCHIZOPHRENIA Chris Frith and
    Eve Johnstone
SCHOPENHAUER Christopher Janaway
SCIENCE AND RELIGION
    Thomas Dixon
SCIENCE FICTION David Seed
THE SCIENTIFIC REVOLUTION
    Lawrence M. Principe
SCOTLAND Rab Houston
SEXUALITY Véronique Mottier
SHAKESPEARE'S COMEDIES Bart van Es
SHAKESPEARE'S SONNETS AND
    POEMS Jonathan F. S. Post
SHAKESPEARE'S TRAGEDIES
    Stanley Wells
SIKHISM Eleanor Nesbitt
THE SILK ROAD James A. Millward
SLANG Jonathon Green
SLEEP Steven W. Lockley and
    Russell G. Foster
SOCIAL AND CULTURAL
    ANTHROPOLOGY
    John Monaghan and Peter Just
SOCIAL PSYCHOLOGY Richard J. Crisp

SOCIAL WORK Sally Holland and
    Jonathan Scourfield
SOCIALISM Michael Newman
SOCIOLINGUISTICS John Edwards
SOCIOLOGY Steve Bruce
SOCRATES C. C. W. Taylor
SOUND Mike Goldsmith
THE SOVIET UNION Stephen Lovell
THE SPANISH CIVIL WAR
    Helen Graham
SPANISH LITERATURE Jo Labanyi
SPINOZA Roger Scruton
SPIRITUALITY Philip Sheldrake
SPORT Mike Cronin
STARS Andrew King
STATISTICS David J. Hand
STEM CELLS Jonathan Slack
STRUCTURAL ENGINEERING
    David Blockley
STUART BRITAIN John Morrill
SUPERCONDUCTIVITY
    Stephen Blundell
SYMMETRY Ian Stewart
TAXATION Stephen Smith
TEETH Peter S. Ungar
TELESCOPES Geoff Cottrell
TERRORISM Charles Townshend
THEATRE Marvin Carlson
THEOLOGY David F. Ford
THINKING AND REASONING
    Jonathan St B. T. Evans
THOMAS AQUINAS Fergus Kerr
THOUGHT Tim Bayne
TIBETAN BUDDHISM
    Matthew T. Kapstein
TOCQUEVILLE Harvey C. Mansfield
TRAGEDY Adrian Poole
TRANSLATION Matthew Reynolds
THE TROJAN WAR Eric H. Cline
TRUST Katherine Hawley
THE TUDORS John Guy
TWENTIETH-CENTURY BRITAIN
    Kenneth O. Morgan
THE UNITED NATIONS
    Jussi M. Hanhimäki
THE U.S. CONGRESS Donald A. Ritchie
THE U.S. SUPREME COURT
    Linda Greenhouse
UTILITARIANISM
    Katarzyna de Lazari-Radek and
    Peter Singer

UTOPIANISM Lyman Tower Sargent
THE VIKINGS Julian Richards
VIRUSES Dorothy H. Crawford
VOLTAIRE Nicholas Cronk
WAR AND TECHNOLOGY Alex Roland
WATER John Finney
WEATHER Storm Dunlop
THE WELFARE STATE David Garland
WILLIAM SHAKESPEARE
    Stanley Wells

WITCHCRAFT Malcolm Gaskill
WITTGENSTEIN A. C. Grayling
WORK Stephen Fineman
WORLD MUSIC Philip Bohlman
THE WORLD TRADE
    ORGANIZATION Amrita Narlikar
WORLD WAR II Gerhard L. Weinberg
WRITING AND SCRIPT
    Andrew Robinson
ZIONISM Michael Stanislawski

Available soon:

PERCEPTION Brian J. Rogers
SOUTHEAST ASIA James R. Rush
BIG DATA Dawn E. Holmes

MIRACLES Yujin Nagasawa
ANALYTIC PHILOSOPHY
    Michael Beaney

For more information visit our website

www.oup.com/vsi/

Andrew Davies

PROJECTS

A Very Short Introduction

OXFORD
UNIVERSITY PRESS

OXFORD
UNIVERSITY PRESS

Great Clarendon Street, Oxford, OX2 6DP,
United Kingdom

Oxford University Press is a department of the University of Oxford.
It furthers the University's objective of excellence in research, scholarship,
and education by publishing worldwide. Oxford is a registered trade mark of
Oxford University Press in the UK and in certain other countries

First edition published in 2017

Impression: 1

Published in the United States of America by Oxford University Press
198 Madison Avenue, New York, NY 10016, United States of America

British Library Cataloguing in Publication Data
Data available

Library of Congress Control Number: 2017942396

ISBN 978-0-19-872766-8

Printed in Great Britain by
Ashford Colour Press Ltd, Gosport, Hampshire

For my mum, Ann,
and
daughters, Abi and Hannah

Contents

Preface xvii

List of illustrations xix

1 Introduction 1

2 America's venture into the unknown 19

3 From Manhattan to the Moon 39

4 Arup's adhocracy and projects in theory 62

5 Lean, heavy, and disruptive projects 83

6 London's megaproject ecology 103

7 Back to the future 127

Further reading 137

Index 147

Preface

Like many things we do at work and in our daily lives, making this book was a project. It started with an idea. There are some excellent books on project management, but too often they provide 'how-to' guidebooks and simple recipes of best practice tools, techniques, and procedures. Each project is treated as a lonely endeavour that can be managed in isolation from the environment within which it is planned and executed. I had recently joined The Bartlett Faculty at University College London (UCL) as Professor of the Management of Projects and wanted to introduce a wider audience to the new thinking about how projects are organized. This theoretically informed approach—sometimes called project studies—seeks to understand how projects adapt to complex, uncertain, and rapidly changing conditions and examines projects in their rich and varied organizational, institutional, and historical contexts. I turned my idea into a proposal, submitted it to a potential sponsor (Oxford University Press), and after some revisions received a contract to produce a book that met the sponsor's specifications. Like many projects, this one was delayed (I missed several deadlines), but was produced within budget (it was a fixed price). In the long term, the success of my project is uncertain: it depends on whether the outcome produces lasting benefits and value for the customer—you the reader.

The outcome is my responsibility, but like most projects this one involved a team of collaborators. I thank Mark Dodgson, David Gann, and David Musson for encouraging me to develop *A Very Short Introduction* to projects and Jenny Nugee and her colleagues at OUP for being so patient and supportive during the execution of my writing project, even when I missed another deadline. My thanks go to managers I have collaborated with in project-based organizations and high-profile projects and to colleagues and students at UCL and elsewhere who continue to make this such a rewarding and stimulating topic which has become the centre of my professional life. I thank those colleagues who provided detailed comments and valuable suggestions for how to improve the book, including Mark Dodgson, Tim Brady, Sam MacAulay, Jonas Söderlund, and Sylvain Lenfle, and those with whom I have co-authored articles and worked most closely with in recent years, particularly Andrea Prencipe, Jennifer Whyte, Nuno Gil, Niels Noorderhaven, Lars Frederiksen, Jens Roehrich, Eugenia Cacciatori, Stephan Manning, Ilze Kivleniece, and Paul Nightingale. I thank colleagues at UCL Donna Cage, Brian Collins, Juliano Denicol, Andrew Edkins, Jim Meikle, Stefano Miraglia, Beth Morgan, Peter Morris, Alex Murray, Natalya Sergeeva, Hedley Smyth, and Vedran Zerjav for clarifying issues and helping with specific questions. Thanks to Mark Thurston, Tim DeBarro, John Pelton, and Sam MacAulay for the creative work and fun we had developing an innovation programme for London's Crossrail project. My gratitude goes to Hans Jörg Gemünden and Carla Messikomer for leading, supporting, and enthusing members of the project studies community. I especially acknowledge Peter Morris, Ray Levitt, Bent Flyvbjerg, and Aaron Shenhar—scholars with a deep appreciation of theory and managerial practice who have had a profound influence on my thinking about projects.

List of illustrations

1   The challenge of managing
    project trade-offs has always
    been with us **4**
    www.CartoonStock.com.

2   Innovative Dibble cranes **30**
    New York Public Library.

3   The finished Deep Cut of the
    Erie Canal **32**
    New York Public Library.

4   Western Development Division
    and Ramo-Wooldridge
    organization **48**
    Adapted from T. P. Hughes, *Rescuing
    Prometheus* (New York: Pantheon
    Books, 1998).

5   Functional, project, and
    matrix organizations **53**

6   The Sydney Opera House **63**
    State Archives NSW.

7   Dongtan East Village **64**
    Courtesy of Arup.

8   Working Together **89**
    © The Boeing Company.

9   Heathrow Terminal 5 during
    construction **104**
    © LHR Airports Limited see
    photolibrary.heathrow.com.

10 Crossrail's tunnelling
    machine **108**
    Anthony Devlin/PA Archive/PA
    Images.

11 Forms of project
    organizing **111**

Chapter 1
Introduction

We depend on projects to transform the natural environment and create the human-built world. We have participated in projects since people first lived and worked in the villages, towns, and cities of the earliest agrarian societies. Projects were established to coordinate work undertaken by temporary groups of people involved in one-off tasks ranging from small informal activities such as hunting and building shelter, to very large and elaborate endeavours such as military campaigns, foreign expeditions (each new voyage overseas was a project), and the construction of buildings, roads, ports, and entire cities. The world's great ancient projects—the pyramids of Egypt, irrigation schemes in Iraq, the temples, aqueducts, roads, and bridges of Imperial Rome, the Great Wall of China, and Gothic cathedrals, for example—were massive in scale, involved enormous numbers of people, and often took years, decades, or even longer to complete.

Today projects are literally everywhere. Complex, one-off endeavours using advanced technology such as the $100 billion International Space Station, Avatar (the first film to go on wide release shot entirely in 3D), and Shanghai's 500 km per hour magnetic levitation train are more obvious examples of projects. The products we use in our daily lives, such as cars, cameras, smartphones, and pharmaceuticals drugs, all start out as projects before being produced in high volume. Many things we do to create change in organizations, think up new ideas and implement them (e.g. an entrepreneurial start-up for customized 3D printing), or respond to emergencies (e.g. humanitarian aid provided by NGOs in a war-torn region of the world) are projects. While they may differ in purpose, scale, and scope, and span many industries, each project is established to bring together people with diverse knowledge to complete a temporary assignment, solve a complex problem, or turn a novel idea into reality.

What is a project?

The word 'project' in the modern sense only came into common use during the 20th century. Before that, it had several different meanings. The *Oxford English Dictionary* finds the word being used in the 2nd century. In classical Latin, the verb *prōiect* means to throw forth or cast away. It was in the 15th century that the word was used to refer to the act of conceiving an idea, proposing a plan, putting something into action, or venturing into the unknown. Daniel Defoe used the word in the title of his book *An Essay Upon Projects* (1697) to describe a 'projecting age' when ventures in foreign expansion and trade, and innovative improvements in science, art, and manufacturing, were being proposed and executed through projects, in pursuit of profits, and 'adventured on the risk of success'.

This *Very Short Introduction* defines a project as a combination of people and other resources brought together in a temporary organization and process to achieve a specified goal. What distinguishes projects from all other organizational activities—such as manufacturing and services—is that a project is finite in duration, lasting from hours, days, or weeks to years and in some cases decades. Unlike manufacturing or service firms, which are presumed to be permanent, a project organization is temporary and disposable by design. Each project brings together people and resources needed to accomplish a goal and disappears when the work is completed. When firms like Bombardier, Siemens, and

Toshiba set out to win contracts for a fleet of high-speed intercity trains, for example, they create a project organization to coordinate work undertaken by their own staff and a network of subcontractors. The organization has a planned life of only a few years and dissolves after accomplishing the job.

Projects range in size from small teams to large international joint ventures and temporary coalitions of public and private organizations. Each one of them has a life cycle with a beginning and an end. Each undertakes a sequence of distinct, but often overlapping, phases or activities to conceive and promote the idea, prepare a proposal and develop a plan, and undertake and complete the work. For example, when Ericsson, the Swedish mobile communications producer, sets out to win a contract from a global mobile network operator (e.g. Vodafone or T-Mobile) it establishes a team with diverse expertise (e.g. technology, services, and sales) borrowed from various units of the firm. The team works to gather information and anticipate the operator's requirements for next-generation mobile systems even before the operator requests bids. When the operator issues a formal invitation to tender, the pre-bid team is disbanded. Many of its members return to their units and a new team is assembled to write the actual proposal. Once the proposal is submitted, the proposal-writing team is dissolved and a new team is established to execute the project. Some individuals move along with the project joining each successive team, but others with specialized expertise are brought in to work on only one or two phases.

A clearly defined project goal and progress toward the goal has traditionally been measured by the three constraints of cost, time, and quality—the so-called 'iron triangle' of project management. The job of the project manager is to complete the project on time, within budget, and according to the desired quality and performance specifications. Trade-offs between time, cost, and quality are often made to meet a project's goal (Figure 1). For example, although

" We had to cut corners ! "

1. The challenge of managing project trade-offs has always been with us.

the time available to construct the venues for the London 2012 Olympics Games was fixed—it was an 'immoveable deadline'—cost and quality could be manipulated to achieve the desired outcome. Too often, however, trade-offs are made without taking into account their impact on customer satisfaction—the 'fourth constraint'—and longer-term strategic objectives.

We now recognize that project success is multidimensional and varies over time. Other dimensions include whether the project develops the knowledge and skills of people, teams, and organizations involved and whether it contributes to an organization's commercial success, profitability, and market share. Projects considered unsuccessful in the short term (measured in cost, time, and quality) may provide new knowledge about technologies, products, services, and customer requirements that open up future business opportunities. As the Sydney Opera House illustrates, great projects considered short-term failures by the triple constraints model can be successful in the longer term if the outcome creates additional benefits and a lasting legacy for owners, users, communities, and even entire countries (Box 1).

4

Box 1 Sydney Opera House

The Sydney Opera House project was originally estimated in 1957 to cost just over $7 million (Australian dollars: AUD) and scheduled to be completed by January 1963. The building was eventually opened in October 1973 (over ten years later than originally planned) at a cost of $102 million (AUD)—a staggering 1,400 per cent over budget. During planning and construction, the project faced a great deal of opposition and criticism. By the time it opened, it was said that the building could not function as a major opera house because the original design had to be changed so many times to accommodate new requirements, cost increases, and delays. Measured against time, cost, and quality objectives, the project would be considered an abject failure, setting a possible world record for poor performance. Yet today the Sydney Opera House—with its roof structure resembling luminous sails—is admired as one of the world's most distinctive buildings. In *Great Planning Disasters* (1980), Peter Hall stated that 'It *is* Sydney' and 'put the city on some sort of mental map of great world cities' (p. 138).

Project managers are responsible for establishing a well-defined plan and then managing the plan until the project is completed. They define the project goal, establish checkpoints, schedules, time estimates, and resource requirements. They manage, motivate, and empower individual members of a project, facilitate communication and build agreements that vitalize teams, and encourage innovation, risk taking, and creativity. Alan Randolph and Barry Z. Posner identify ten simple principles to help managers plan and manage projects (see Table 1). When projects are complex, unpredictable, and changing, plans have to be flexible and projects adjusted to situations that cannot be foreseen at the outset. Managers of uncertain projects have to iteratively plan/manage, plan/manage until they accomplish the goal.

Table 1 Principles for planning and managing projects

Planning projects

1. Set a clear project goal	Start at the finish and work backward. Setting a project goal involves the sponsor, project manager, the project team, and the users of the project.
2. Determine project objectives	Establish detailed objectives to help members of the project understand how their contributions relate to the overall goal.
3. Establish an action plan and time estimates	Create an action plan to detail what is going to be done and how you will monitor your progress towards project completion.
4. Draw a picture of the project schedule	Draw a picture or a schedule of the project to visualize project activities, relationships among activities, and time estimates.

Managing projects

5. Direct people individually and as a project team	Develop a strong team of collaborators, encouraging them to learn from experience, and to expose and solve problems.
6. Reinforce team commitment	Encourage people to join a project where they feel a sense of ownership and are committed to its success.
7. Keep everyone connected	Overcome barriers to communication, keep people informed on a regular basis, listen and use information brought to them by team members.
8. Build agreements that vitalize team members	Projects require the coordination of tasks and integration of different units and people. Conflict can be a force for imagination and creativity.
9. Empower yourself and others on the project	Project managers need power arising as much from individual competence as from formal authority. Managers of high-performing projects share power.
10. Encourage innovation, risk taking, and creativity	Plan for innovation. Sharing ideas and creativity requires support and communication. Innovation is reinforced by goals, budgets, and deadlines.

The need to adjust to changes in the environment explains why a project can achieve its goal, but still result in failure. For example, Motorola's $5 billion Iridium project was a fixed-price contract (a price set at the start that remains unchanged through to completion) to build a constellation of satellites providing voice and data communications for satellite phones. It could be considered a success because it was completed on time, within budget, and satisfied the technical specification, but was a failure in commercial terms. While the project was under way, Motorola's management team failed to see that rapidly expanding terrestrial mobile phone networks which we now all depend on would completely undermine Iridium's satellite-based business model.

A project can be complete in itself such as the creation of a new consumer product, building, or urban metro system. It can form part of a continuing programme of interrelated projects using shared resources and coordinated to achieve a common objective such as the nationwide rollout of a mobile communication system. A portfolio can be established to allocate resources to a set of projects that are planned, mapped, and sequenced to achieve an organization's long-term strategic objectives such as Apple's digital hub of products and online iTune services (Chapter 5).

Projects and operations

A distinction is made between projects and operations. Projects perform novel, non-repetitive, one-off tasks and produce unique, one-off, or customized outcomes for individual customers, such as a building, change programme, or new airport. Operations undertake ongoing, repetitive tasks and produce standardized products and services in high volume for mass markets, such as cars, computers, and fast-food meals. Projects are a flexible and adaptable way of organizing, dealing with individual client requirements, and promoting innovation when conditions are turbulent and fast-changing, whereas operations are designed to perform standardized routines in a stable and predictable environment. We will discover, however, that projects vary in complexity, pace, and uncertainty (Chapter 4) and perform tasks ranging from unique to repetitive (Chapter 6).

A distinction is also made between the outputs and outcomes of projects. Outputs are the tangible and intangible things a project creates such as a building, IT system, or organizational process. Outcomes are the results or benefits created for the sponsor, customer, and user when the project becomes operational, such as improved performance, enhancements to existing products, and the creation of new markets.

There is a transition between project and operations when outputs (e.g. a new fleet of trams) are handed over and translated into operational outcomes (e.g. a functioning urban tram system). As the project moves to completion, components and subsystems have to be integrated, tested, and end users have to learn how to operate the outputs (hardware, software, and services) before the project becomes operational.

Many complex projects fail because of unsuccessful transitions. A timely and seamless operational transition is more likely if there is a strong sponsor presiding over the project and the operator is embedded at an early stage, articulating its requirements and deeply involved in all preparations for opening. Take for example the chaotic opening of Terminal 5 at London Heathrow Airport in March 2008 when many flights were cancelled and baggage was delayed and misplaced over a period of twelve days. Learning from this misguided attempt to open a complete terminal in one go, the airport operator decided to prepare for the 'soft opening' of Terminal 2—the next major construction project at Heathrow. A dedicated 'operational readiness' team was embedded in the project organization two years prior to the official opening on 4 June 2014. A successful handover was achieved by opening the terminal in stages including 180 trials with 14,000 volunteers,

1,700 training sessions, a digital 'mock-up terminal' to assess check-in software, a test with a live flight, and staged process to move each airline into the live terminal building.

Some projects extend into the provision of operational services and can last many years. For example, Alstom Transport (a division of French-based Alstom) was awarded a £429 million Private Finance Initiative contract (see Box 3) in 1995 to renew the fleet of trains on the London Underground's Northern Line. Rather than specify the exact size of the fleet, the London Underground requested an outcome: it required that 96 trains be available for service each day over a period of twenty years. To achieve this target, Alstom produced 106 trains and established a dedicated maintenance organization to service them. Demand for projects that include the provision of services has encouraged many project-based firms—IBM, Alstom, and Rolls-Royce—to change their entire business models so that they can both design and integrate systems *and* provide services to operate and maintain them.

All organizations engage in projects to a greater or lesser degree, but the activities of some organizations and industries are almost entirely based on projects, such as Airbus's aeroplane business, IBM's information technology solutions, and Zaha Hadid's architectural practice. For project-based organizations, each new customer order constitutes a new project, whereas high-volume producers like Sony, Samsung, and Starbucks, and large government agencies, rely on projects alongside their operations to implement strategies, develop new products, create organizational change, build new assets and systems, and deal with one-off problems or opportunities.

A brief history of projects

Alvin Toffler introduced the word 'adhocracy', popularized in *Future Shock* (1970) and *The Third Wave* (1980), to describe a new species of post-industrial organization: temporary, ad hoc, and adaptive project groups and teams. Toffler argued that the invention of agriculture associated with the first wave was brought to an end by a second wave initiated by the British industrial revolution in the late 18th century and subsequent rise of mass production in the United States and Germany. A third wave, initiated in the mid-20th century, is based on the radically new principles of post-industrial information society. Toffler believed that temporary project structures and access to information made possible by the invention of the computer would overwhelm the previous social arrangement and counter the standardization of tasks, bureaucracy, hierarchy, and other second-wave values and interests.

Many construction projects of the agrarian age were accomplished by the 'master builder'. Combining the roles, knowledge, and practical experience of architect, engineer, and craftsman, the master builder was responsible for generating new ideas and turning them into reality, designing the building, and employing craftsmen to construct it. Sir Christopher Wren, for example, was appointed as chief architect after the Great Fire of London in 1666 to survey the damaged area, plan the new city, design the buildings including St Paul's Cathedral, and manage construction.

This bond between design and construction was broken around the time of the industrial revolution when engineering and architecture evolved into specialized scientific and elite professions, largely segregated from the rest of the building trade. With the establishment of elite professional civil engineering bodies in France in the late 17th and 18th century, engineers assumed responsibility for the design, specifications, and procurement of bridges, roads, and other government projects and for defining the tasks performed by contractors during their execution. Professional civil engineers appeared later in the UK. After the Institution of Civil Engineers was founded in 1818, the engineers that designed the roads, canals, and railways—Thomas Telford and Isambard Kingdom Brunel, for example—became organizationally and contractually separate from those that built them. Thomas Brassey's general contracting firm, for instance, constructed much of Britain's railway network. After the foundation of the Royal Institute of British Architects in 1834, architecture was established as a profession and architects were prohibited from engaging in profit-making contracting. The designer of the building subsequently became disconnected from engineering and the daily practice of construction. In recent years, architects, civil engineers, and product designers—such as Frank Gehry, Ove Arup, and Thomas Heatherwick—have attempted to re-establish the role of master builder to preside over projects in a collaborative process linking design closely with construction (Box 2).

Until the mid-20th century, the most widely practised and advanced form of project management was found in construction. Yet projects were ignored as a form of organization by industrial

Box 2 Project maker and master builder

Thomas Heatherwick's London design studio is a 'project maker'. It experiments with new materials, develops new ideas, and produces innovations ranging in scale from products (e.g. a new fuel-efficient London bus) to the design of iconic buildings (e.g. the UK Pavilion at the 2010 World Expo in Shanghai) and shape of future cities. As Heatherwick emphasizes, generating new ideas and making them happen means that each project 'is an intense mixture of certainty and doubt, breakthroughs and dead ends, tension and hilarity, frustration and progress'. The studio works as a collection of overlapping projects; each one is formed around a client's problem and led by an experienced member of the studio. Influenced by the historical figure of the master builder, Heatherwick believes the separate roles of the architect, craftsman, engineer, and designer should be combined in a collaborative team so that the design of a product or building is closely connected to the process of turning it into reality.

society's scholars and practitioners. Instead they focused on understanding how improvements in operations—stretching back to the railways and the birth of the modern corporation—gave rise to the large, hierarchical, and permanent organization. Max Weber, the German sociologist and the era's leading theoretical proponent, argued that there was one best way of organizing large groups of people. Rules about the breakdown of work, top–down authority, and large-scale bureaucratic structures were designed to perfect standardized operating procedures and improve performance in a stable environment. Frederick W. Taylor's scientific management and Henry Ford's Model T assembly line put some of these ideas into practice. Mass production became the key to the growth and competitive survival of corporations such as Ford, Standard Oil, Carnegie Steel, and Coca-Cola. Volume producers integrated backwards into sources of raw materials and component manufacturing and forwards by buying distributors and controlling channels to mass markets.

Management theory and practice had little or nothing to say about projects where an entirely different organizational logic prevailed. In a fascinating essay on projects in economic history, Philip Scranton notes that the railways were held up as a model that other organizations should emulate, but the question of how they 'could be operated at a profit overshadowed issues of how they could be built in the first place'. This is surprising because the British and American industrial revolutions could not have occurred without large-scale endeavours organized through projects: the construction of canals, railways, telegraph, and telephone networks carrying large volumes of raw materials, people, information, and goods; the factories, plants, and machinery of mass production; the energy, lighting, water, sewer, and other utility systems; and the built environment of rapidly urbanizing societies. Almost everything was contracted out to multiple independent parties working jointly on a shared activity in a temporary organization that disappeared on completion of its task. Projects created something one-off and unique, whereas running the completed outcome was a continuing operation.

The key historical turning point was during and after the Second World War when management scholars and professional managers began to recognize the importance of projects in the defence and aerospace industries (Chapter 3). The challenges involved in developing America's technologically advanced weapons systems—particularly the Manhattan Project that produced the atomic bomb and the Atlas and Polaris ballistic missiles—called for a radically new and more sophisticated way of managing complex projects. The 'systems approach' created for these projects encouraged managers to focus on understanding the whole system, including the interfaces and interconnections among components. New forms of project organizations, processes, and tools were established to bring together, schedule, and coordinate scientists, engineers, and managers working in multidisciplinary project teams.

The systems approach to project management spread in the 1960s and 1970s to many other industries in the United States and elsewhere in the world. In his book *Rescuing Prometheus* (1998) on post-war American technological projects, Thomas Hughes suggested that the systems approach to project management is as significant as:

> the spread of scientific management in the early twentieth century under the aegis of Frederick W. Taylor and his followers. Taylorites, however, applied scientific management techniques to ongoing manufacturing operations rather than projects.

By the 1980s, many organizations that had previously focused on improving their operations were finding it difficult to adapt to an increasingly turbulent, uncertain, and fast-changing environment. Some began to search for more flexible ways of dealing with ceaseless change, rather than seeking to control it. As Toffler wrote in *The Adaptive Corporation* (1985), the adhocracy emerged because:

> A 'one-time' or temporary problem, however, requires a 'one-time' or temporary organization to resolve it. It is obviously inefficient to build a full, permanent structure to deal with a problem that will not be there after a fixed interval of time. The result is a necessary proliferation of modular, temporary, or self-destruct units—task forces, problem-solving teams, *ad hoc* committees, and other groups assembled for a special and temporary purpose.

In their book *In Search of Excellence* (1982), Tom Peters and Robert H. Waterman expected the adhocracy to spread to new industries and environments that were becoming more uncertain, complex, and demanding of innovation, even penetrating the largest and most successful bureaucratic organizations of the 20th century, such as IBM and General Electric. In the expanding middle ground between firms and markets of the post-industrial information society, Manuel Castells emphasized that the unit of production '*becomes the business project enacted by network*, rather than individual companies or formal groupings of companies' (original emphasis).

The adoption of the project form accelerated in the 1990s when the diffusion of personal computers, the Internet, world wide web, the smart phone, social media, and other digital technologies began to reshape all forms of work. Boeing, for example, chose a 'paperless' approach using computers to design, test, manufacture, and integrate the 777 aeroplane project (Chapter 5). Digital technologies are now widely used to support activities undertaken during the entire project life cycle and often continue into the operation and maintenance of an asset. In our Internet-enabled world, digital information can be shared in real time by participants with access to a smart phone or laptop computer working collaboratively in almost every type of project.

In the 21st century, projects are the vehicle for sustaining an organization's existing activities, but they play an even more fundamental role as the engine of innovation—from idea to commercialization—in a globally competitive market. The world's most competitive firms use projects to develop new technologies, design innovative products, processes, and services, introduce organizational change, launch internal corporate ventures, and implement business strategies. As product life cycles become shorter, firms have to accelerate the development of new and diverse products and services before existing offerings become obsolete, particularly in fast-paced and highly competitive consumer markets. Large firms are increasingly honeycombed into projects in a move to create flexible, problem-solving structures focused on innovation. Some mass producers are outsourcing the volume manufacturing parts of their vertically integrated operations and focusing on being 'project orchestrators' of a network of external manufacturers and suppliers involved in new product development. BMW and Renault treat each new product platform, the basis for the next family of vehicles, as a project. Nike no longer makes running shoes; it manages footwear projects. Coca-Cola outsources bottling and marketing of drinks and is now run more like a collection of projects.

Changes in government procurement policy, privatization, and the opening up of state sectors to competition have resulted in a great proliferation in the number and types of public projects such as university research, highways maintenance, schools, housing, hospitals, airports, concert halls, urban railway systems, water waste, flood defence, and sustainable energy projects. These changes have created new opportunities for public and private organizations, often working in partnership, to take on the risks and responsibilities of projects in the public sector, subject to social obligations, resource conservation, and environmental protection (Box 3).

In a recent book, Rolf Lundin and his co-authors describe a trend, beginning in the 1960s, when the share of operations in

Box 3 Public–private partnerships

In the 1990s, the UK pioneered new forms of contracts for public projects. The Private Finance Initiative (PFI) requires that the private sector design, build, finance, and operate projects and receive payments spread over many years or decades. In contrast to PFI where the private sector finances projects and assumes much of the risk, the Public–Private Partnership (PPP) finances public projects partly from the private sector, while government shares or underwrites some of the risk. In 2013, for example, the UK's National Health Service had over 130 PFI/PPP projects worth £12 billion. The largest PFI hospital project was awarded to Capital Hospitals, a private consortium. Under the £1.1 billion contract, Capital Hospitals is responsible for designing, building, redeveloping, and maintaining two new London hospitals until 2048 on the sites of St Bartholomew's and Royal London hospitals.

organizations began to decline and the proportion of projects started to increase rapidly. World Bank data on fixed capital formation (expenditure on construction works, machinery, and equipment) in 2015 provides a rough indicator of a class of economic activity undertaken mostly as projects: 23 per cent of the world's $114 trillion expenditure on gross domestic product is fixed capital formation and in some newly industrializing countries the figure exceeds 30 per cent—31 per cent in India and 46 per cent in China. Much of this investment is delivered by 'megaprojects': large-scale, complex, and high-risk scientific, engineering, or infrastructure projects that cost $1 billion (established at 2003 prices) or more. With spending on global megaprojects at $6 to $9 trillion annually, Bent Flyvbjerg believes this is 'the biggest investment boom in human history'.

The growth of project organizing is likely to be even more pervasive than these figures suggest. It is spreading beyond new product development and traditional project-based industries that always produced one-off and customized products and services (e.g. defence, aerospace, construction, consultancy, software, media, and entertainment) to almost every corner of post-industrial society. Consumer goods suppliers, government organizations, universities, schools, non-governmental organizations, 'pop-up' fashion or retail shops, volunteer groups, charities, and many other organizations now depend on projects to create innovation, break away from established patterns, solve complex problems, and explore entrepreneurial opportunities.

Project performance

Organizations in the 21st century continue to improve their standardized operations through lean production, business process re-engineering, quality management, six sigma, and other management innovations. They have not been so successful with projects. Despite the growth in the number and the opportunities to improve performance by learning from experience, projects often fail to achieve their cost, time, quality, and longer-term objectives.

Several influential studies provide an indication of the poor performance of projects since the late 1950s. In a review of the publicly available reports on project overruns published between 1959 and 1986, Morris and Hough found that around 3,500 projects in a variety of industries from around the world experienced overruns of between 40 and 200 per cent. Shenhar and Dvir's data on over 600 projects in private, public, and non-profit sectors in various countries found that 85 per cent of projects failed to meet their original time and cost objectives: with an average overrun of 70 per cent in time and 60 per cent in cost. Poor performance does not just affect the stakeholders directly involved in a project. The prosperity of cities and even countries can be affected by the failure of a single project. The cost overruns and debt resulting from the 2004 Olympic Games in Athens, for example, were so large they severely weakened the Greek economy.

As we will discover in the rest of this *Very Short Introduction*, what is common to most of these poorly performing projects is that they failed to adapt to the environment. Project sponsors, executives, and managers have to define the purpose and appreciate the conditions—the complexity, uncertainty, and time available to complete the task—at the start and adapt to unforeseen situations as the project progresses. Projects have a past to learn from and a future to create. Too often they are treated in isolation from previous projects and the wider historical and organizational context within which they are conceived and executed.

In Chapter 2, we will find that large-scale engineering endeavours were delivered, often very successfully, long before the formal tools, language, and discipline of project management were available.

Chapter 2
America's venture into the unknown

America's most ambitious and largest engineering project of the early 19th century faced challenges that managers of today's megaprojects would recognize. When the project was conceived, however, there were no professional civil engineers or managers in the United States with the knowledge required to organize such a large and complex endeavour. The project created knowledge where no such capability existed before and where many unknown conditions would have to be faced and overcome. It became its own school of engineering and a training ground for project managers. It was the key to America's industrial future. The project was the Erie Canal.

The goal of the project was to create the world's largest inland waterway connecting New York with Lake Erie. For many years the project was considered wildly unrealistic. In 1809 President Thomas Jefferson considered the construction of the canal through America's internal wilderness as 'little short of madness'. Peter Bernstein writes that the idea of a massive artificial inland waterway binding the east to the western frontier of the nation 'appeared as fantastic as sending a rocket to the Moon'. The project had to overcome the enormous physical challenges such as traversing rivers, dense forest, malarial swamps, valleys, and rock escarpments. It had many champions, but was fiercely contested right up to and many years after funds for its construction were approved in 1817. Despite these obstacles, the project was completed on time, close to the original cost estimate, and opened for service on 26 October 1825.

The Erie Canal created a channel for an increasing flow of raw materials, grain, and produce to the Hudson River at Albany in the east and almost unlimited supplies of goods and people to travel to the Niagara River at Buffalo in the west. The 363-mile (584-kilometre) inland waterway was over thirteen times longer than America's largest canal. The canal was 4 feet deep (1.2 metres) and 40 feet wide (12.2 metres) with 83 locks made of stone so that boats could rise and fall a total of 675 feet (206 metres) along its entire course over 18 aqueducts. It inspired the construction of a 3,300-mile network of canals—America's first mass transportation infrastructure.

The project was funded, designed, and managed by government and succeeded where private canal ventures had tried and failed. A group of elected New York politicians defined the goals of the project, set the political stage, secured funding, and oversaw the canal's design and construction. They appointed surveyors with no civil engineering experience—but with a willingness to learn and a talent for innovation—to identify the route, develop the design, estimate the costs, solve technological problems, and plan and inspect the work. In what today we might call a public–private partnership, the project was managed by a temporary public body and undertaken by private contractors selected by competitive tender to build short stretches of canal under the direction of state-employed engineers.

Conception and promotion

The idea of an interior route for a canal between the Hudson River and Lake Erie taking advantage of the Mohawk River gap—the only water-level route through the Appalachian Mountains—was conceived by New York politicians and wealthy speculators long before construction began in 1817. If the canal could be built, it would unlock the immense natural resources of America's west and bring them through New York City on freight-laden barges at a fraction of the costs incurred over land routes. One of the earliest proposals to improve inland navigation along this route was put forward by Sir Henry Moore, governor of New York, in 1768. But like many subsequent proposals it failed to gather the political support required to develop the idea.

The Western Inland Lock Navigation Company was formed in 1792 to make improvements on the Mohawk River. Although the Western Company lacked the engineering expertise needed to navigate larger natural obstacles along the river, the work undertaken indicated that an inland waterway through the Appalachian Mountains might be possible. Many of the leading engineers and politicians later involved in the Erie Canal project worked for the Western Company. The company was short of private finance and badly managed, but it provided an important lesson for those who went on to create the Erie Canal: a project this large would have to be managed and financed by government.

The first concrete proposal for the Erie Canal can be traced to fourteen essays written in 1807 and 1808 by Jesse Hawley, a New York grain merchant. Hawley explored different designs, technological options, and routes for the canal. He considered possible sources of funding and suggested that the canal be built with federal money rather than private finance, which he dismissed as inadequate, monopolistic, and self-interested. Based on his readings about the dimensions, complexity, construction time, and the cost of major European canals, he predicted that the canal would cost $5 million to build. Completed in 1681, the Canal du Midi connecting the Atlantic Ocean and the Mediterranean Sea across south-western France demonstrated that it was possible to build a canal on a massive scale—although the Erie Canal was more than twice as long as the French one. A few months later, after reading about France's Canal du Midi and Scotland's Clyde canals, Hawley's revised figure of $6 million accounted for the additional costs of his favoured design concept—an inclined plane design with twenty-six locks falling from the elevation of Lake Erie to Mohawk. Hawley's estimates about the costs and benefits of the canal proved to be incredibly accurate. The project which started a decade later was publicly funded, based on roughly the same cost estimate, and followed a route similar to the one he suggested.

Those promoting the canal were concerned that New York's ascendancy as a commercial centre was under threat. The journey west was difficult through the great physical barrier of the Appalachian Mountains and easier routes were available further south. Baltimore, Philadelphia, and other cities were growing rapidly because they were connected by turnpike from Pittsburgh to Philadelphia and the national road to Baltimore. The burgeoning trade route from the Mississippi and Ohio rivers to the Gulf of Mexico threatened to hand commercial supremacy to New Orleans. The Erie Canal's supporters were convinced that an inland waterway was required to establish New York as America's main gateway to western markets.

In the first legislative step toward the building of the canal, federal government provided the modest budget of $600 to conduct a survey of the most direct route for the canal between the Hudson River and Lake Erie. The survey was undertaken in 1808 by James Geddes—a young and inexperienced surveyor who went on to be chief engineer on the western section of the Erie Canal. His 1809 report anticipated the future layout and design of the Erie Canal, including a series of locks and a great embankment to scale the forested ridge at what became Lockport.

Inspired by Hawley's essays, De Witt Clinton first began supporting the Erie Canal project in 1810. During his long political career, Clinton served as United States senator, mayor, and governor of

New York. He threw his political weight behind the project and risked his career in turning it from a dream into a reality. Clinton was named as a member of the Canal Commission of New York State in April 1810. So important was his role in the project that some would call it Clinton's 'Big Ditch'.

Clinton and the other commissioners championed the Erie Canal in a highly uncertain and contested political environment. Politicians representing southern states and cities actively resisted a scheme that would increase the commercial strength of New York. Many of those who would eventually benefit most—New York politicians and residents along the route—actively opposed the canal until it opened for service. The commissioners had to negotiate with many stakeholders along the canal's route and convince those who were openly hostile to the construction of the canal, including powerful politicians, residents, and the New York press. The commissioners built momentum behind the project by attracting popular support for a scheme few thought could be built. In 1815 and 1816, Clinton organized mass public demonstrations for canal supporters in New York City and a populist campaign—collecting thousands of signatures—to support a memorandum to the legislature demanding that the project be approved.

The commissioners' efforts to gain approval and funding for the project depended on detailed surveys of the route and an estimation of the construction costs. In the summer of 1811, the commissioners appointed Benjamin Wright—a surveyor with some experience of canal construction gained while working for the Western Company, who was later appointed chief engineer for the middle section of the canal. In 1816 Wright and Geddes conducted in-depth surveys of alternative routes to Lake Erie and considered various design concepts to prepare for construction the following year. On the basis of these surveys, the commission raised the total cost of building the canal from $5 million to $6 million.

The commissioners were empowered to seek financial support from Congress as part of a programme of infrastructure investment in national road and canal projects. Federal funding was preferred because other private canal ventures, such as the Western Inland Navigation Company, had ended in failure. But the federal government was reluctant to fund a massive public project that represented New York's interests, particularly in a period of economic instability, rising public expenditures, and trade restrictions imposed during the Anglo-American War. Despite attracting political allies and support in Congress, the Erie Canal was unable to secure federal funding when, in 1816, President James Madison used his constitutional right to veto the bill. After this option was closed, the commissioners were forced to seek funding from the New York state government. The state legislature asked the commissioners to come up with recommendations on how to raise the $6 million needed to build the canal. This was a huge amount of money at the time, equivalent to almost a third of all the banking and insurance capital in New York state.

The commissioners' report published in February 1817, complete with maps and profiles, recommended a canal following a northern route that was 353 miles long with seventy-seven locks (slightly shorter and with fewer locks than the eventual outcome). They rejected the inclined plane design and used the same dimensions and shape as the 27-mile (44-kilometre) long Middlesex Canal connecting the Merrimack River with Boston. Apart from this, there were no other American examples to prepare for such a massive and complex endeavour. Based on a construction estimate of $13,800 per mile, they reduced the total estimated costs of construction from $6 million to just under $5 million, primarily to make the expenditure more agreeable to the New York legislature.

Construction of the Erie Canal was finally approved on 15 April 1817 when a Canal Bill was passed by the New York state government. A new group of five commissioners including Clinton were responsible for overseeing the construction of the canal, which was largely financed by selling state government bonds to the public and financial markets abroad, particularly British investors. As significant as the project's technological achievements, this innovation—the Canal Fund—in public finance was widely adopted to fund other canal projects. Efforts to attract extra funding continued while construction was under way. By 1824 the state government and commissioners had sold nearly $7.5 million in canal bonds.

Design and construction

After gaining government approval and securing funding, those championing the canal now had to decide how to achieve the objectives of the Canal Law of 1817. As governor of New York and president of the commission, a position he held until 1824, Clinton was the project's main sponsor responsible for attracting support and overcoming political obstacles encountered during the execution of the project. Two acting commissioners were appointed to manage the day-to-day activities of the project: Samuel Young as the commission's secretary and Myron Holley as the commission's treasurer. Benjamin Wright and James Geddes became chief engineers responsible for the design and construction of the canal. With no formal training as engineers and little or no knowledge of canal construction, they had to learn as they went along.

The commissioners' 1817 report, which synthesized the previous surveys and design considerations, became the construction blueprint for the Erie Canal. The 363-mile canal was built between 1817 and 1825 in three sections with engineers and contractors assigned to each. The middle section extended about 94 miles (151 kilometres) from the Mohawk to Seneca rivers. Work began with a ground-breaking ceremony on 4 July 1817. Facing fewer natural obstacles, construction of this relatively flat section was finished in October 1820. The experience and new techniques devised to build this section proved valuable when the project moved on to the far more difficult western and eastern sections which began in parallel in 1819. The 110-mile (177-kilometre) eastern section along the Mohawk River was finished in the autumn of 1823. When the 160-mile (257-kilometre) western section to Lake Erie was finished in 1825 the entire canal was integrated as a complete system and ready for operation.

Wright and Geddes assembled a group of inexperienced young men to undertake detailed surveys of each section of the canal, notably John Jervis, Nathan Roberts, and Canvass White, who would go on to become America's leading engineers and canal builders. They had to establish design specifications for each section, estimate the costs of construction, and plan the schedule of work. The original plans, design, and route layout had to be adjusted to address difficulties encountered when the project was under way. At Clinton's request, but using his own money, White visited Britain in 1817 to study canals, tunnels, underwater cements, and aqueducts. After visiting Thomas Telford's Pontcysyllte Aqueduct built on iron arches a hundred feet above the River Dee in North Wales, White understood how bold and innovative engineering design could overcome the most difficult natural obstacles. When he rejoined the project in 1818, he was more knowledgeable about canal engineering than almost anyone in the United States and contributed greatly to the design and construction of locks, dams, and bridges on all parts of the Erie Canal.

Whereas simple excavation was the main work on the middle section, tackling the eastern and western sections called for far more advanced engineering solutions. On the eastern section, the lower Mohawk Valley required twenty-seven locks over 30 miles (50 kilometres) to climb over a series of natural rapids including the Cohoes and Little Falls. On the western section, an 802-foot (244-metre) stone aqueduct carried the canal over the Genesee River at Rochester. An even more imposing natural obstacle had to be overcome on the far western end of the canal. The commissioners invited several engineers to submit plans to scale the ridge of solid rock on the Niagara Escarpment. They chose the design proposed by Nathan Roberts: two flights of five locks—one flight for the eastern route and one for the western route—to climb the 66-foot (20-metre) limestone ridge at the new town of Lockport. Constructed in four years, this landmark structure was the most remarkable feat of engineering on the entire Erie Canal.

The commissioners met in June 1817 to design the project organization and contractual approach used to employ and manage the canal builders. They decided to let out construction work to multiple private contractors. Each of the three sections of the project was broken down into smaller, more manageable components—a practice widely used on today's large engineering projects. A contractor was employed to build a stretch of canal—as short as a quarter of a mile (about 400 metres) and no longer than 3 miles—under the supervision of canal engineers employed by the state. Contracting out work in small stretches had been used on a small scale on the Middlesex Canal, but the Erie Canal promoted and perfected the practice. Each contractor was effectively responsible for building a miniature canal largely in isolation from canals constructed by other contractors on either side. Building the canal in short stretches meant that the risks of employing contractors with little or no experience in canal construction were limited by the size of each contract. It was a risk the commissioners believed worth taking in a state with limited resources and no experience in public construction projects.

The use of competitive tendering—now widely used on government projects—was considered novel in a period when canal labourers were traditionally employed directly by the state. Contractors were compensated for the risks incurred and received extra payments for overruns due to changes in the scope of work (such as the decision to use stone rather than wood in the aqueducts) or additional work required to deal with unexpected problems (such as the great flood of 1817). They were not supposed to receive payment until the work was completed and inspected by an engineer. Few had the financial resources to pay for the tools, provisions, and horses required to undertake the work. So the commissioners offered contractors monthly advances of up to $2,000, with a final payment made on completion of the work, less advances. Safeguards were put in place to suspend in-progress payments and enforce strict compliance when a contractor was found to be corrupt or covering up mistakes. A contractor who failed to start the work, complete it on time, or meet the required specifications had to repay the advance with interest. Some less reputable contractors sought to earn extra profits by making questionable claims for extra work that were often hard to reject. In most cases, however, the relationship between the commissioners and contractors was less formal and often more collaborative. The difficulty of settling contractors' accounts upon completion of their work was eventually solved by ensuring that any changes in the scope of work were openly and frankly discussed, documented, and settled as formal written contract variations.

Competitive tendering helped keep the project on schedule, but the cost of constructing some of the more challenging parts of the canal exceeded the original estimates. Completed on time in 1820, the middle section cost about $1 million and was only about 10 per cent over budget. The more difficult Genesee aqueduct was finished in September 1823, eleven months behind schedule and $83,000 over the original cost estimates. By 1821, however, the commissioners were able to reduce the overall cost of canal construction because of the large number of contractors bidding for work at reduced prices. While some contractors failed, others successfully developed and honed their skills and capabilities as they completed one contract after another. For example, John Richardson, the canal's first signed contractor, went on to become one of the largest contractors on the entire project.

There was one exception to this policy of employing private contractors. The excavation work on the 'Deep Cut'—through 3 miles of solid limestone and another 4 miles through a mixture of rock and earth extending south-west from the brow of the ridge at Lockport—was originally let out to private contractors in four stretches. This was the most difficult part of the western section. Work began in 1821 but proceeded slowly. By September 1823 the commissioners decided that the task was beyond the capabilities of private contractors and would have to be undertaken as a public works project. Thousands of employees were hired by the state to blast and cut their way through the rock under the direct control of canal engineers.

To make a profit from contracts awarded to the lowest bidder, contractors had to develop numerous innovations—new processes, tools, and materials—to complete the project efficiently and deal with unexpected problems that might delay it or push it over budget. Many innovations were developed by workers with the least training and experience, but who were willing to conduct repeated experiments until they got it right. Several new tools were developed soon after work began on the middle section. Contractors responded to the extraordinary flooding of 1817, which made work much harder than expected, by creating a new canal excavation technique. Operated by three people and a team of horses or oxen, the 'plough and scraper' was used to sever and remove small roots. Developed in 1818, the 'tree-felling' machine operated by one person was used to clear larger areas of forest. For trees cut down in the traditional way, by axe or saw, a 'stump puller' operated by seven men and horses was developed to remove residual stumps and roots.

Constructing a canal through the difficult terrain and mountainous obstacles on the western section required even more significant innovation. A new device called the 'Dibble Crane' was developed when it became impractical and inefficient to continue removing large volumes of excavated material from the Deep Cut by small

PROGRESS OF EXCAVATION, LOCKPORT.

2. Innovative Dibble cranes used to excavate the Lockport Deep Cut section of the Erie Canal.

wheelbarrows. This massive wood-framed crane used a large bucket raised and lowered by rope and pulley to excavate the material as quickly as it accumulated (Figure 2).

Ronald E. Shaw writes that the discovery of waterproof cement was 'one of the epochal achievements of the building of the Erie Canal' because it gave birth to the American cement industry. Canvass White is often credited with discovering a quicklime cement that hardened under water after conducting repeated experiments with varieties of local limestone. Abundantly available and easily prepared, this waterproof lime was used to construct the entire Erie Canal, reducing costs and eliminating the dependence on imported European cement. White took out patents on his original innovation in 1820 and on an improvement in 1821. Initially the Erie commissioners regarded the discovery as their intellectual property and encouraged contractors to supply the cement without payment of royalties. But White was eventually successful in winning the suit and defending attempts to purchase his patent rights.

Opening and outcome

When the canal opened, the whole nation celebrated America's mastery over nature—a symbol of progress that united political leaders, militia, traders, industrialists, and the general public. Clinton was voted out of office in 1822 and removed from the Canal Board of Commissioners in 1824. But he benefited from the great excitement and increasing popular support for the canal as it approached completion. He was re-elected as governor of New York in time to preside over the grand opening ceremony in Manhattan when he poured a keg of water from Lake Erie into the Atlantic Ocean to mark the 'Wedding of the Waters' on 4 November 1825.

The Erie Canal was the longest canal in the world, built with the least experience, and provided benefits that exceeded the most optimistic predictions (Figure 3). It must be considered a success in the terms we now use to evaluate project performance. It was completed on schedule on 26 October 1825, at a cost of $7.1 million that was surprisingly close to the original estimates, and without experiencing a significant failure or delay during construction. The accuracy of the original estimates is extraordinary given the novelty of the task and uncertainties involved in traversing dramatic and abrupt changes in elevation, manoeuvring the towering Niagara escarpment, and clearing and digging through large areas of forest. Most of the designs worked precisely as planned and many innovations were successfully deployed to keep the project on track and within budget. The state's debt was paid off in less than a decade.

The Erie Canal project did much more than construct a 363-mile ditch connecting western territories to New York. It propelled

DEEP CUTTING, LOCKPORT.

3. The finished Deep Cut of the Erie Canal, 1825.

the rise of America as an industrial nation. The volume of east–west trade more than doubled in the first year of the canal's operation. The costs of transporting goods from Buffalo to New York City dropped from $100 to less than $10 per ton. The flow of revenues quickly exceeded the canal's operating costs.

By 1833, the tolls charged on the canal repaid the cost of building the canal. The economic growth generated by the canal exceeded the aspirations of those involved in promoting it, accelerating western migration, stimulating urban development along the banks of the canal, and opening up new markets for the flow of goods and people to the Midwest and large volumes of grain and raw materials to New York and Europe. Benefiting from America's first east–west trade link, New York quickly became the Empire State and commercial centre of a new global power.

The Erie Canal project was a learning experience for engineers who went on to design and build America's canals and railways in the 19th century. With no engineering training available in the United States, building the canal became the so-called 'Erie

School of Engineering' with Wright and Geddes as its deans. Wright developed a reputation for building canals and railways in Canada, Cuba, and the United States and received the posthumous honour of 'Father of Engineering' awarded in 1969 by the American Society of Civil Engineers mainly for his work on the Erie Canal. Geddes went on to design canals in Ohio, Pennsylvania, and Canada. Some of the most notable graduates of the Erie School became the greatest American civil engineers of the 19th century. Canvass White left the Erie Canal before its completion to become chief engineer of Pennsylvania's Union Canal. John Jervis and Nathan Roberts went from canals to design America's railways.

Implications for the management of projects

The Erie Canal raises fundamental issues about the management of large, complex, and uncertain projects. A project starts with an idea, vision, or proposal. If the idea is taken forward, a project sponsor defines the goal, explores alternative designs, estimates the costs and benefits, secures funding, identifies the uncertainties facing the project and how they can be overcome, and plans a schedule of work with demanding but achievable targets. After securing funding and gaining approval, an organization has to coordinate and schedule work undertaken by multiple contractors. In large projects, the work is divided up into manageable chunks (which we now call the 'work breakdown structure') and undertaken in phases that are completed sequentially, but can overlap or occur simultaneously. A project ends and an operational activity begins when the newly constructed facility is used to provide a service.

The Erie Canal illustrates what Peter Morris has emphasized: a project is more likely to be successful if the sponsor (owner and operator of the asset) spends time at the beginning—in the 'front end'—defining the goals, understanding the benefits and risks, and shaping the strategic approach. The sponsor has to engage with multiple stakeholders (e.g. politicians, users, contractors, local businesses, and the public) whose interests, expectations, and concerns may be impacted positively or negatively by the performance and outcome of a project. The difficult task of setting a goal should involve a dialogue between the sponsor, project manager, and end users to clarify what they want from the project.

Although we should not underestimate the vital role played by De Witt Clinton, the success of the Erie Canal, like most engineering projects, is attributable to the judgement and insights brought into play by the leadership group rather than any single individual. The project had many champions: visionary thinkers who first proposed the idea; commissioners who shaped the project, secured funding, and gained approval in the face of strong political opposition; acting commissioners who managed and pushed the project through to completion; and engineers and contractors who were able to overcome the huge technological challenges facing the project.

The Erie Canal is an example of a large-scale engineering endeavour which we would now call a 'megaproject' (Chapter 6). In their efforts to gain approval and secure funding, sponsors frequently underestimate the costs, risks, and completion times and overstate the benefits of a megaproject. Bent Flyvbjerg and his colleagues have shown that the tendency to underestimate the costs—'optimism bias'—can be avoided in the planning stage by learning from other comparable projects. Although no canal project in the world was as large and complex as the Erie Canal, studies of other canals and detailed surveys of the route did help to obtain a realistic estimation of the costs and risks involved. The final cost was deliberately underestimated—this is what Flyvbjerg calls 'strategic misrepresentation'—to make the project more attractive as an investment to the New York legislature.

Ultimately the project was delivered on time and almost within budget. Perhaps more importantly, the benefits far exceeded the most wildly optimistic expectations of Hawley, Clinton, and other promoters.

Despite the opportunities to learn from large-scale endeavours undertaken over the two centuries that have passed since the Erie Canal, most of today's megaprojects are late, over budget, and fail to meet their original goals. In a study of sixty large engineering projects around the world, Miller and Lessard found that 40 per cent of the projects were inefficient in terms of cost, time, and technical performance, over 18 per cent had extensive cost overruns, and nearly 27 per cent had long schedule overruns. In a study of 258 railway, fixed-link, and road megaprojects, Flyvbjerg and his co-authors found that cost overruns of 40 per cent are common and overruns of 80 per cent are not uncommon. In an article published in 2014, Flyvbjerg found that nine out of ten megaprojects have cost overruns of up to 50 per cent. Table 2 provides a list of megaprojects with huge cost overruns, but let's consider one in more detail.

The Boston Central Artery/Tunnel (CA/T) was America's largest and most expensive civil engineering project at the time of its construction. Boston's 'Big Dig' was originally scheduled to open in 1998 at an estimated cost of $2.6 billion. The project involved a 7.5-mile (12-kilometre) new highway system with tunnels and bridges to improve the flow of traffic through the Boston region with links to Logan International Airport. Design and construction was managed by the state-owned Massachusetts Turnpike Authority, and a joint venture between Bechtel and Parsons Brinckerhoff coordinated the multiple contractors involved in the project. These organizations confronted many technical, geological, political, and environmental problems that had not been accounted for at the outset and called for modifications and creative ways to resolve them as the project

Table 2 Large-scale projects have a calamitous history of cost overrun (adapted from Flyvbjerg 2014)

Project	Cost Overrun (%)
Suez Canal, Egypt	1,900
Scottish Parliament Building, Scotland	1,600
Sydney Opera House, Australia	1,400
Montreal Summer Olympics, Canada	1,300
Concorde Supersonic Aeroplane, UK, France	1,100
Troy and Greenfield Railroad, USA	900
Excalibur Smart Projectile, USA, Sweden	650
Canadian Firearms Registry, Canada	590
Lake Placid Winter Olympics, USA	560
Medicare transaction system, USA	560
Bank of Norway headquarters, Norway	440
Furka Base Tunnel, Switzerland	300
Verrazano Narrow Bridge, USA	280
Boston's Big Dig Artery/Tunnel project USA	220
Denver International Airport, USA	200

Projects

progressed. CA/T was finally completed eight years behind schedule in December 2007 and cost about $15 billion: after adjustments are made for inflation this is a cost overrun of about 220 per cent.

Inadequate front-end planning, strategic misrepresentation, optimistic behaviour, and escalating commitment to a failing cause are some of the reasons why megaprojects perform so badly. But megaprojects also fail because the organizations involved are unable to adapt plans and innovate when conditions change unexpectedly and new opportunities arise during their execution. Albert Hirschman introduced the principle of the 'Hiding Hand' to explain how innovative resources are brought into play to deal with uncertainties not foreseen when planning large-scale projects, particularly those with long gestation periods, when unexpected problems arise much later and require more serious efforts to resolve them. Challenging projects are undertaken, Hirschman argued, because we misjudge 'the nature of the task, by presenting it to ourselves as more routine, simple and undemanding of genuine creativity than it will turn out to be'. It is better not to know the real costs involved. An invisible hand hides the difficulties from us and helps get projects started.

We now know that the Hiding Hand principle is overly optimistic about the downstream innovative capacity of megaprojects to solve problems overlooked by upstream planners. Yet it does at least help us to recognize the potential for applying innovation at every point in the life cycle to complete megaprojects more efficiently, as the Erie Canal case illustrated. Innovation in the front-end stage is enhanced by learning from other contexts and how similar projects elsewhere in the world are designed, financed, and organized. Since megaprojects are rarely executed and completed as originally planned, the parties involved have to find ways of resolving problems and innovating as they go along.

The Erie Canal marked the beginning of long and close association between engineering and project management. The rapidly industrializing countries in Europe and North America depended on large technological systems—canals, railways, and telegraphs—that could not be designed and constructed without well-developed engineering and project management capabilities working in unison. Already established as a profession in France and the UK when the Erie Canal project started, civil engineering would acquire a similar status in the United States as a formally recognized discipline and soon be widely taught in American universities. Project management would have to wait until the 1960s before it would receive similar attention and recognition.

Chapter 3
From Manhattan to the Moon

The Panama Canal, Henry Ford's River Rouge automobile production plant, the Hoover Dam, Tennessee Valley Authority complex, and Empire State Building are some of the great early 20th-century projects that would shape America's future. Like the Erie Canal, these projects accomplished their goals long before project management was established as a formal discipline. The real breakthrough in the management and organization of large, complex projects, however, can be traced back to the Second World War Manhattan Project, which developed the atom bomb, and the early post-war Atlas Project, which produced the intercontinental ballistic missile. With few precedents to guide them, new structures, processes, and tools had to be created to coordinate, schedule, and integrate the vast networks of people, resources, and organizations involved in these projects. To accelerate progress, multiple systems were developed in 'parallel' and phases of research, design, testing, and production were undertaken simultaneously—or 'concurrently'—rather than sequentially. Scientists now collaborated closely with engineers and managers in interdisciplinary teams. Dedicated organizations with 'project managers' and 'systems engineers' were created for each project. As the Soviet threat intensified during the Cold War of the 1950s and 1960s, increasingly complex and technologically advanced systems had to be designed and produced at rapid pace. Originating in the Atlas and subsequent missile projects before migrating to the Apollo space programme, a new 'systems approach' was established to manage the immense proliferation of technological projects.

Manhattan Project

The goal of the Manhattan Project was to produce the atomic bomb and bring the Second World War to a successful completion more quickly than was possible by conventional warfare. By the summer of 1945 when its mission was accomplished, the original $6,000 authorized in February 1940 to initiate research on fission chain reaction had increased to an expenditure of $2.2 billion. The project was unprecedented in its concentration of human and physical resources dedicated to the production of a single product and comparable in size to the American automobile industry. At its peak, this geographically dispersed government-led project employed about 130,000 scientists, engineers, managers, and workers to achieve an urgent goal in the utmost secrecy under the command of President Franklin D. Roosevelt and a few senior Cabinet officers.

In 1939, Albert Einstein wrote a letter urging President Roosevelt to support the development of 'extremely powerful bombs', fearing that the United States might fall behind Germany in the race to develop the military potential of atomic energy—the idea that immense quantities of energy would be released if fissionable materials (either uranium-235 or the recently discovered plutonium-239) could be developed to cause a nuclear reaction. A great release of energy occurs when fissionable materials break down (fission) more quickly than they can escape from an assembly. In response, Roosevelt established an advisory committee to oversee a programme of research to produce a fuel source of fissionable material for a nuclear explosion.

The Manhattan Project was formally established in June 1942 when it became clear that a vast array of laboratories, production plants, and reactors would have to be constructed at multiple locations to produce the bomb. Most of the early research was undertaken by Columbia University in the Manhattan District of New York where the army established the 'Manhattan Engineering District'. As a result, the project became known as the Manhattan Project even though it was geographically dispersed at sites across the country with plants in the states of Tennessee, Washington, and New Mexico and university research laboratories in Columbia, Chicago, Virginia, and Berkeley.

In September 1942, General Leslie Groves—an experienced engineer who had recently overseen the construction of the Pentagon, the largest building in the world at the time—was appointed to lead the project. The United States Army Corps of Engineers with its vast experience in large-scale construction projects was responsible for materials procurement, engineering design, and construction of the plants and facilities. Stone & Webster had already been appointed in spring 1941 as principal contractor for the project, bringing its knowledge of engineering, consulting, finance, and large-scale construction. On 28 December 1942 President Roosevelt approved a budget of over $2 billion to build full-scale processing plants to supply large quantities of uranium and plutonium explosives and design the bomb. Formal contracts were made with large industrial corporations such as Eastman Kodak, Du Pont Company, General Electric, and Westinghouse to design, construct, and operate the laboratories, plants, reactors, and processing equipment of the nuclear-production system.

With ample funds available, completing the project in less than three years was more important than saving money. At such an early stage, it was not possible to foresee which technology would eventually prevail. The military's preference for a production line of atomic bombs was not feasible. Given the limited supply of fissionable material, only one or two bombs would be built. To have a chance of completing the project as quickly as possible,

Groves and his advisory committee decided that two bomb designs (uranium and plutonium) and three processes to produce fissile material should be pursued in parallel. As Groves put it: 'The whole endeavour was founded on possibilities rather than probabilities.' There was no certainty which bomb design would work or which fissionable explosive material would be required for each bomb.

Initially two processes for uranium-235 isotope separation—electromagnetic and gaseous diffusion—were installed at Oak Ridge, Tennessee. The 70-square-mile (180-square-kilometre) Oak Ridge complex was carefully selected because of the availability of electric power, water supply, and railway connections, and the remoteness of the location helped maintain secrecy. After making insufficient progress with these processes, Groves decided that a third process—thermal diffusion—should be investigated and it was this process that was eventually selected for the preliminary separation of uranium.

The only process available to produce plutonium was a reactor pile of uranium and graphite blocks. Plutonium research was undertaken at the Metallurgical Laboratory of the University of Chicago. In order to set production schedules and determine plant capacity, Groves needed to know how much plutonium would be required for each bomb. But in autumn 1942, he discovered that the Chicago scientists had no accurate idea of the quantities of plutonium needed and compared his position to 'a caterer who is told that he must be prepared to serve anywhere between ten and a thousand guests'. With such limited scientific and technical data, Groves decided to press ahead 'at full speed' with plutonium production despite the possibility of failure. In December 1942 Du Pont Company was contracted to design, construct, and operate plutonium production piles and separation plants. In February 1943, Groves acquired another large and remote site at the Hanford Engineer Works, near Pasco, Washington, to build three large-scale production piles, or reactors, and four plants for separating plutonium. Du Pont faced the challenge of freezing the engineering designs and proceeding with construction (involving 42,000 people during the peak period) using experimental and incomplete data supplied by the Chicago Lab.

While waiting for fissionable uranium and plutonium material, parallel efforts were under way to design the atomic bomb. In 1942, the physicist Robert J. Oppenheimer was appointed as head of the Los Alamos Scientific Laboratory to lead the research and development (R&D) team of scientists responsible for combining fissionable material to achieve a nuclear explosion and designing bombs that could be dropped from a plane and detonated in the air above the target. A seminar organized by Oppenheimer in July 1942 identified as many as five different bomb designs. The various design solutions were explored in parallel before two designs were selected: the 'gun design' for the uranium bomb, the 'implosion design' for the plutonium bomb. To preserve the open communication and traditional independence of scientists, Los Alamos initially adopted a functional department structure organized by academic disciplines. By the spring of 1944, however, the project was in crisis when tests showed that the plutonium gun assembly bomb design failed to work. Finding that the development of the more complex implosion bomb design was proceeding too slowly, Oppenheimer decided to create a dedicated project organization focused on the end product to improve communication, facilitate cross-functional integration, and instil a greater sense of urgency.

Small quantities of the uranium and plutonium material eventually arrived from Oak Ridge and Hanford respectively, the implosion design was frozen in February 1945, and by the summer of that year the two bombs were assembled. With insufficient material available for testing, the uranium bomb utilizing the gun method, known as 'Little Boy', was shipped directly to operations in the Pacific region. There was enough plutonium available to test the 'Fat Man' plutonium bomb named after Winston Churchill and for another bomb to be used against Japan. A field test was undertaken because there was less confidence in the performance of the plutonium bomb and reliability of the implosion method. The world's first atomic bomb was exploded in a test facility near Albuquerque in New Mexico on 16 July 1945.

The project achieved its primary goal of producing the atomic bomb and bringing the war to an end as early as possible. The uranium bomb was dropped on Hiroshima on 6 August 1945. It killed 70,000 people on impact and another 70,000 died by the end of 1945. The plutonium bomb was dropped on Nagasaki on 9 August 1945. It killed 40,000 people and the death toll reached 70,000 by January 1946. The Japanese offer to surrender was announced on 10 August.

According to General Groves, the project was 'successful'—despite the catastrophic consequences—because it had a clearly defined mission (even though how the goal would be accomplished was entirely unclear at the outset), the work was divided up into specific tasks, and authority was delegated to the right level of responsibility. The Manhattan Project set a precedent for parallel development on post-war missile projects by developing two bomb designs and several processes of fissile production simultaneously. It benefited from extensive trial-and-error learning from parallel trials of alternative technologies and designs, progressively resolving uncertainties and taking advantage of unexpected developments while the project was under way.

Atlas Project

After the Second World War, the United States and Soviet Union entered into an arms race to develop increasingly powerful weapons systems. America started Intercontinental Ballistic Missile (ICBM) research after hearing reports about missile projects in the Soviet Union and the explosion of a fusion device in 1953. An ICBM missile consisted of a rocket engine, a giant cylinder of fuel, a nose cone carrying a nuclear warhead, and a guidance and control system. It was designed to follow a ballistic (a gravity-shaped trajectory) flight of about 5,000 miles (8,000 kilometres) at a velocity of over 10,000 miles per hour and deliver a nuclear warhead within 5,000 feet (1,500 metres) of its target.

In 1953, the Air Force established an advisory task force—known as the 'Teapot Committee'—of elite scientists and engineers to oversee ICBM research. It included Simon Ramo and Dean Wooldridge, the founders of the systems engineering firm Ramo-Wooldridge Corporation that would play a major role in the Atlas Project. The committee recommended that missiles should be developed 'to the maximum extent that technology would allow' and made the formal recommendation to President Dwight D. Eisenhower in February 1954 to launch an ICBM programme on a 'crash basis'. Placed at the top of the nation's military priorities, ICBM development was undertaken by the Air Force with few limitations on funding.

America's ICBM programme depended on advances in engineering and project management that were even more tightly connected and focused on solving the 'systems problems' than any previous endeavour. The ICBM programme produced three missiles: Atlas, Titan, and Minuteman. In 1957, during its most intensive design phase, the entire programme involved 18,000 scientists, engineers, and technical experts, 70,000 people in 22 industries, 17 principal contractors, and 200 subcontractors. The first Atlas and Titan test missiles were launched in 1958 and proved feasible for a 5,000-mile flight. Initiated in 1958 and deployed in 1962, the Minuteman missile eventually superseded the Atlas/Titan missiles.

In July 1954, the Air Force established the Western Development Division—located in a vacant church in Ingelwood, near Los Angeles—as a 'special project office' under the leadership of Brigadier General Bernard Schriever (promoted to General soon after his appointment) to develop the ICBM missiles. Schriever is considered to be the father of project management because the 'systems approach' that he created for Atlas—with the help of Simon Ramo and other advisers—was widely adopted to manage many other military, aerospace, and civil projects.

Schriever spent a considerable amount of his time managing key stakeholders 'outside the system' and working across organizational boundaries to secure funding, gain access to senior decision makers, and ensure his managerial initiatives were not handicapped by a slow-moving bureaucratic approval process. But the most pressing task initially facing Schriever was to decide what organization could provide the Air Force with the technical and systems engineering expertise required to coordinate the efforts of numerous participants from industry, government, and universities involved in the Atlas Project. The Teapot Committee recommended the creation of a 'Manhattan-like' project organization, but Schriever rejected this advice because neither the Air Force nor scientists had the technical capability required to manage ICBMs, which were considered even more complex than the atomic bomb.

The Air Force could have resorted to the traditional practice honed during the Second World War of appointing a single airframe manufacturer as 'prime contractor' to design and coordinate the subcontractors involved in the development of the ICBMs. But Schriever was not convinced that any airframe manufacturer had the breadth of capabilities in systems engineering and physical sciences required to develop a broad base of technology extending beyond airframe manufacture and assembly to electronics and computing. After considering various alternatives, Schriever and his advisers decided that a radically new type of organization was required to assist the Western Development Division. Ramo-Wooldridge was assigned to act as 'systems integrator', providing the Air Force with the systems engineering and technical advice required to manage the project.

The configuration of the missile system shaped the organization of the project (Figure 4). A parallel structure was created to facilitate the close interaction between Air Force project officers and Ramo-Wooldridge project managers. Each subsystem of the Atlas missile, such as propulsion and guidance, was assigned its own project officer and project manager. As Simon Ramo described it, all the parties were 'locked into a single integrated project and a single integrated design of the ICBM missile and system'. The physical layout of the building reflected the close cooperation between the two interdisciplinary groups. Ramo and Schriever, as well as their deputies, met frequently and were 'co-located' in adjacent offices in Ramo-Wooldridge buildings.

Ramo-Wooldridge worked alongside the Air Force and together they decided upon the 'associated contractors', coordinated their activities, and monitored their performance. Consolidated Vultee Aircraft Corporation (Convair), which had already been developing a long-range missile called Atlas, was contracted for the final assembly of the airframe. However, Convair's missile had not yet been flight tested and was years away from production. Schriever discussed the challenge of developing such unproven ICBM technology with General Groves and Oppenheimer and decided to adopt the practice used on the Manhattan Project of developing systems in parallel. The Glenn L. Martin Company was contracted in October 1955 for the final assembly of a backup system, the Titan missile, using alternative airframe technology. Each major subsystem of the Atlas and Titan missiles—the airframe, guidance, propulsion, nose cone, and computer—was also developed simultaneously by associated contractors to stimulate the search for alternative technical solutions and assure that the failure of one contractor could not delay the project (Table 3).

As the systems integrator on the Atlas Project, Ramo-Wooldridge's staff of a hundred or so civilian engineers and scientists were able to see interconnections among parts of the whole system. Guided by a common vision, they were responsible for optimization of the

47

Projects

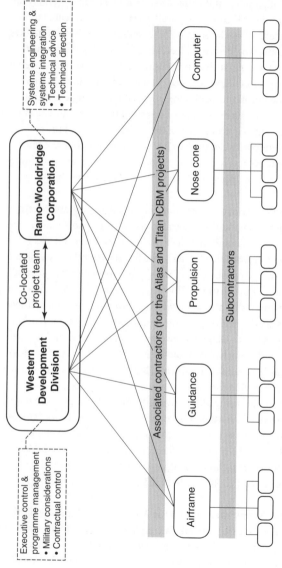

4. Western Development Division and Ramo-Wooldridge organization.

Table 3 Associated contractors for the Atlas and Titan ICBM projects

Subsystem	Atlas	Titan
Airframe	Convair	Martin
Guidance *Radio-inertial* *All-inertial*	General Electric A.C. Spark Plug	Bell Telephone American Bosch and MIT
Propulsion	North American	Aerojet General
Nose cone	General Electric	AVCO
Computer	Burroughs	Remington Rand

Source: T. P. Hughes, *Rescuing Prometheus* (New York: Pantheon Books, 1998).

entire system, which involved making trade-offs among its component parts that could reduce the reliability, range, or accuracy of each missile. Developing a lighter warhead, for example, involved a trade-off that reduced the propulsion, or thrust, requirement of the ICBM. Ramo-Wooldridge's systems engineers prepared background studies, produced preliminary designs, and defined specifications for the performance of each subsystem and the interfaces between them. Designs were considered 'preliminary' until they were finalized, incorporated in working drawings, and used to produce prototypes of missile components and systems. If specifications for components or subsystems changed during the project, Ramo-Wooldridge engineers modified the affected parts in the missile system to achieve a compatible match. After that, they controlled the test and operational environment within which the missile was put to work.

After specifications were defined and produced as working drawings, Ramo-Wooldridge's systems engineers assumed responsibility for the technical direction of the Atlas Project, working closely with Schriever's project officers to select the contractors and monitor their performance. Contractor selection was a drawn-out process lasting almost three months. It involved ranking potential firms for their technical and management capabilities, inviting the highly ranked firms to bid, evaluating their proposals, and selecting the preferred contractor. General Electric, for example, was selected as the nose cone contractor for the Atlas missile and AVCO Manufacturing Corporation for the Titan missile. Schriever and Ramo held what were known as 'Black Saturday' meetings with their project officers and project managers in a control room with an early digital computer displaying real-time information supplied by contractors to deal with cost overruns, delays to scheduled milestones, and failures to meet performance standards during tests.

Schriever believed that the traditional 'serial' approach to develop subsystems in sequential phases would be too slow to win the ICBM race with the Soviet Union. In serial development, research led to design, which led to prototype development, testing, and production of the weapon, which led to maintenance and training methods to use it. To accelerate development, each activity had to be undertaken in overlapping phases. The term 'concurrency' was coined by Schriever to explain the process and justify why it was needed. Under concurrency, the design and test facilities started before the details of the test programme were finalized. Work on the assembly and launch facilities at Cape Canaveral, Florida, for example, started before the missile's size, shape, performance, and operational specifications had been determined. Years later Schriever qualified that concurrency is a prerequisite for large systems projects when 'time is of the essence' because of the attendant risk of costly duplication and massive coordination failure.

Coordinating the concurrent development and testing of components and subsystems was one of the most difficult tasks facing the Atlas Project. Systematic planning and scheduling was required because subsystem and interface designs could not be frozen until preliminary specifications were defined for related parts of the system. Specifications could not be finalized until extensive research and testing had been completed on individual subsystems and the interactions between them. Ramo-Wooldridge's systems engineers developed procedures for progressively freezing the design to reduce the 'ripple' effect of corrective and costly design alterations. Configuration management procedures were created to ensure that any proposed design changes were reviewed and signed off by a Change Control Board and communicated to all affected parties.

Convair's role in the Atlas Project illustrates how contractors shifted from dedicated project organizations to a new type of matrix structure. In 1954, Convair created the Astronautics division to undertake work for the Atlas Project. The number of staff working on the project increased from 300 in 1953 to 9,000 in 1958 and to 32,500 in 1962. During most of the 1950s, Convair ran Atlas as a single-project organization, but soon experienced priority problems and conflicts of authority in its functional departments when it began to develop different versions of Atlas and initiate new subsystem projects, such as the Azusa tracking system. The Astronautics division addressed this problem by creating a matrix organization with a director for each programme working with project and functional managers to schedule tasks and resolve priority issues. By 1963, every one of Astronautics major new programmes was organized as a matrix to sustain and manage the growing number of projects (Box 4).

Pioneered by Schriever, Ramo, and others, the systems approach created for the Atlas Project helped achieve the programme's goal—to win the race with the Soviet Union to develop the first operational ICBM missile. A similar story could be told about the Navy's Polaris Programme under the leadership of Admiral William F. Raborn. The Navy established a Special Projects Office (SPO) to develop and integrate Polaris fleet ballistic missiles for use on board submarines. Unlike Atlas, however, systems integration on the Polaris Programme was undertaken in-house

Box 4 Functional, project, and matrix organizations

Traditional 'functional organizations' proved unable to cope with the growth in ICBM projects. Communication across separate engineering, manufacturing, sales, and other functional departments was simply too long and cumbersome to provide effective managerial coordination of many large, complex projects.

Contractors like Convair and Martin Company originally established 'project organizations' bringing together people from manufacturing, engineering, research, sales, finance, and other functional departments into groups focused on a single project. A project manager controlled and integrated all of the functional resources required to achieve each project's goal. However, the growth in ICBM work in the late 1950s called for a further organizational innovation.

In the new two-dimensional 'matrix organization', each employee was attached to a functional department and assigned to one or more projects that could not be accomplished by a single department. Members of projects now reported to a functional and a project manager. When their task was accomplished, they returned to their functional home. The matrix structure was designed to accelerate the flow of information, allocate resources more efficiently across multiple projects, and discourage people in functional 'silos' from looking at problems from their own narrow perspective.

Figure 5 provides a simplified illustration of the three structures used to organize projects.

by the Navy's SPO. Polaris also created its own notable project management innovations, such as the Program Evaluation and Review Technique (PERT) network planning tool, run on computers from 1957, to display and provide time estimates for a sequence of planned activities and their anticipated completion dates.

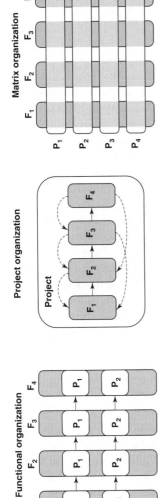

Functional organization

F_1 F_2 F_3 F_4

Project work is coordinated by functional managers and completed sequentially as it passes from one function/department to another

Project organization

Project

$F_1 \rightarrow F_2 \rightarrow F_3 \rightarrow F_4$

A project manager integrates all the functions and work is undertaken sequentially and concurrently in a dedicated, standalone structure (e.g. Convair and Martin Company in the 1950s)

Matrix organization

F_1 F_2 F_3 F_4

P_1
P_2
P_3
P_4

Established to execute multiple projects. Each project is coordinated by a functional and a project manager (e.g. Convair Aeronautics in the 1960s)

Key:
$F_1 - F_4$ Functional departments (e.g. R&D, engineering, manufacturing, and operations) or disciplines (e.g. scientific and engineering expertise)

$P_1 - P_4$ Projects established within an organization

→   Sequential development of project work in stages

----   Feedback from later to earlier stages in concurrent development

5. Functional, project, and matrix organizations.

53

However, PERT contributed surprisingly little to the success of the Polaris programme. It was primarily used to allow technical development to take place unhindered by excessive interference from outside politicians and officials.

Apollo Moon landing

The influence of the systems approach benefited enormously from the establishment of the National Aeronautics and Space Administration (NASA) in 1958 and the first Apollo Moon landing on 20 July 1969. In 1961, the Soviet Union announced that it was winning 'the space race' with the United States when it launched Yuri Gagarin into space. President John F. Kennedy responded in May that year by stating that 'this nation should commit itself to achieving the goal, before this decade is out, of landing a man on the Moon and returning him safely to the Earth'. Starting with almost no knowledge of how people function in a weightless state, NASA designed and built a system incorporating many new technologies—rockets, spacecraft, test facilities, life-support systems, and a computer-controlled tracking and communications network—that would place men on the Moon in less than a decade. The final cost of over $20 billion for the Moon landing was close to the original estimate of $13 billion plus a contingency of $7 billion. Captured visually with television broadcasts, Apollo sold the benefits of the system mode of project management to the world.

James E. Webb, Head of NASA's entire Space Programme, believed that the first Apollo Moon landing mission faced even more profound managerial challenges than the Manhattan Project. NASA had to coordinate 300,000 staff working for 20,000 contractors and 200 universities in 80 countries. The Apollo programme was led by NASA in collaboration with the space-system divisions of several large contractors—such as General Electric, Lockheed, and Boeing. While subsystem development work was undertaken by contractors, NASA had to retain sufficient systems integration capabilities in-house to know more about the whole endeavour than any individual contractor.

Project management ideas and practices pioneered on Atlas, Polaris, and other missile projects were transferred to the Apollo programme when staff working on these projects joined NASA. In September 1963, George Mueller, formerly of Thompson-Ramo-Wooldridge (TRW), became head of NASA's Office of Managed Space Flight. Mueller joined the programme after the key design choices had already been made. But he soon discovered that the chances of achieving a Moon landing before 1970 were no more than one in ten. Mueller created a matrix structure to improve communications and surveillance of the programme: work divided into functions (programme control, systems engineering, flight operations, test, reliability, and quality) was undertaken in the three centres working on manned missions (Huntsville, Houston, and Canaveral). He abandoned the long-drawn-out process of having numerous flight tests and different vehicle configurations and decided instead to have all components developed and ready for 'all-up testing' using the full Apollo flight configuration.

Recognizing that NASA had little capability in planning and managing large programmes, at Schriever's suggestion, Mueller recruited Brigadier General Samuel C. Phillips from his position as director of the Minuteman missile project to become the Apollo Program Director. Phillips and Mueller had to maintain the flexibility required to tackle unforeseen problems, while introducing disciplined systems-based management (e.g. configuration management, change control board, PERT, and systems engineering) to accelerate the programme schedule, control costs, and achieve the 1969 deadline of landing a man on the Moon. Introduced in January 1965, NASA's Program Development Plan, which identified how the programme's schedule and phases would be managed and organized, became one of the main tools of systems-based project management.

In *Space Age Management* (1969), Webb wrote that NASA's Moon landing was successful because the organization created to manage the project was flexible and adaptive with the 'capacity to adjust to and to move forward in an unpredictable and sometimes turbulent environment'. NASA recognized that many of the predictions about Apollo's technology and operating environment would turn out to be wrong and that it had to 'make the most careful analysis of all known factors at the start of a project and still be prepared to adjust when actual conditions turn out to be different from those foreseen'. Webb suggested that 70 or 80 per cent of tasks undertaken by NASA could be known and prepared for in advance with some degree of certainty, but the remaining 20 to 30 per cent represented a zone of uncertainty that had to be addressed by adaptation and innovation when the project was under way. A balance has to be struck, Webb concluded, between 'orderliness and stability' for the known and predictable part of a large, complex project and 'procedures that will foster innovation' for the fluid and uncertain part.

Given the technological uncertainties involved, NASA could not afford to rely entirely on fixed-price contracts favoured by the Department of Defense. Fixed-price contracts specified the task to be performed for a definite quantity of money. They focused attention on the start of a project, when the specifications were defined and the contract was agreed upon, and the conclusion, when the technology was accepted or rejected. But they ignored the need for adaptation to unforeseen contingencies while projects were under way. NASA acknowledged that fixed-price contracts worked well when conditions were known and predictable, but preferred to use incentive contracts for the development of novel technologies, with bonuses for efforts to improve on the original specifications and address unexpected problems and opportunities. For example, Boeing Company had an incentive contract to produce five spacecraft to photograph the Moon on five missions including incentives on cost, schedule, and spacecraft performance in orbit.

This flexible contract encouraged parties to adjust tasks and alter schedules when conditions changed and new information became available (see Chapter 4).

Project management's lost roots

By the end of the 1950s, the new systems ideas and practices circulated informally and began to take hold when individuals involved in the ICBM and Polaris programmes moved on to occupy leading positions on other projects. The foundations of a new discipline called 'project management' were laid when engineers, managers, and academics formally articulated and codified the new approach. Articles began to appear in management journals and when the first project management textbooks appeared in the 1960s they were based on the systems approach. When Robert McNamara became Secretary of Defense in 1960 he reorganized military procurement and established systems-based project and programme management.

Systems-based project management spread quickly in the 1970s to the European space programmes and other industries and government agencies throughout the world. The influence of project management led to the foundation of professional associations in the United States and Europe—the International Project Management Association (IPMA) in 1967, the Project Management Institute (PMI) in 1969, and Association for Project Management (APM) in 1972. Proponents of project management (Box 5) emphasized its practical nature and the need for people trained in project management to implement standardized guidelines, processes, and bodies of knowledge that are universally applicable to all projects, programmes, and portfolios, such as the PMI's Project Management Body of Knowledge (PMBoK).

Despite the achievements of the Atlas and Apollo projects, systems project management experienced difficulties during and after the 1970s when many government-funded military and space projects

Box 5 Standardizing project management

The PMI's *A Guide to the Project Management Body of Knowledge (PMBoK® Guide)* (2013) defines phases of the project life cycle and the processes required to identify client and stakeholder requirements, and ensure that the project is completed on time, within budget, and according to requirements.

A project starts with a plan based on a scope statement including: a work breakdown structure (WBS) defining the packages of work, an organizational breakdown structure (OBS), network schedule diagrams, a budget, and resources. A 'baseline plan' determines how the project will be executed in some detail and provides a fixed target against which the performance of the project team will be assessed. A risk management plan assumes that the uncertainties facing a project can be identified up front and establishes a contingency plan for dealing with them.

Once the project is executed, performance is measured against the baseline plan. Changes to the plan should be kept to a minimum or seen as an exception that needs to be corrected. Execution should conform to the baseline plan for the project to be a success, even though key assumptions in the plan may be rendered invalid when circumstances change.

suffered from severe time and cost overruns and poorly performing outcomes. Projects were often approved and funded without an adequate consideration of technological alternatives that available funds might make possible and without providing well-reasoned objectives based on a realistic estimation of the cost, timing, and performance of each individual project. Some were initiated—such as the Space Shuttle and International Space Station—with too many unknowns to allow accurate forecasts of costs, time to completion, performance, risk to human life, market demand, and usefulness.

NASA's Space Shuttle programme was first proposed in 1969 when the country was still excited by the Moon landing and the possibility of landing a crew on Mars in the 1980s. After its initial expensive proposal received little support, NASA sought to gain government approval by developing a more cost-effective space-adapted aeroplane based on a reusable system and off-the-shelf components. The Shuttle was a recoverable system that was designed to launch a manned space vehicle that would return to Earth and be used on repeated flights. The government decided to concentrate all of its resources on the Shuttle, eliminating alternative technologies such as non-recoverable launch vehicles. As Simon Ramo explains, optimism bias (Chapter 2) shaped efforts to gain approval and funding for the Shuttle:

> NASA based all estimates of cost, time, and performance on the most optimistic of possibilities. Because of this extreme optimism, the Shuttle program and its difficulties started at almost the same time. With the technical problems badly underestimated and the time allowed to complete the necessary steps far too short, the Shuttle's progress quickly slipped behind schedule.

It is highly unlikely the project would have been funded had the original estimates and forecasts on the Shuttle been realistic. Under pressure to minimize costs, NASA had abandoned its original plan to build a small test vehicle to ensure all the technology was proven before embarking on a full-scale vehicle. The Shuttle ran into significant cost overruns and Shuttle flights were cancelled following the Challenger disaster in January 1986 which killed all seven astronauts. Attempts were made to understand the causes of the accident and the Shuttle programme resumed in September 1988. After the Columbia accident in February 2003, which also tragically killed all seven crew members, NASA's Shuttle fleet was grounded until July 2005 and completed its final mission in 2011.

By the late 1960s, there was a widespread belief that the systems approach developed on the Atlas and Apollo projects could be applied to rebuild America's rapidly decaying and congested cities. But it failed to fulfil its promise and proved unable to cope with the immense social, political, and environmental problems of large urban areas. Many believed that America's urban renewal and construction projects were even more complex and messy than putting a man on the Moon. In their fascinating study of the Apollo programme, Leonard R. Sayles and Margaret K. Chandler pointed out that compared with America's urban projects, 'NASA had a simple life. NASA was a closed loop—it set its own schedule, designed its own hardware, and used the gear it designed. It was both sponsor and user. Space was no one's territory.' In contrast to this 'closed system', projects in densely populated urban areas are 'open systems'. During the design of the Boston Central Artery/ Tunnel (Chapter 2), for example, many different voices and stakeholders in the city—federal, state, and local governments and local-interest groups with poverty, ethnic, and environmental concerns—all had a say in shaping a project which was years late and hugely over budget.

The aerospace-generated systems approach used to manage large projects became increasingly discredited from the late 1960s because of its failure to address America's urban problems, its association with the failing military campaign during the Vietnam War, and its contribution to the escalating arms race of the Cold War. Civil rights, anti-Vietnam War, environmental, and nuclear disarmament activists blamed the threat to liberal values, damage to local communities, and destruction of the natural environment on their government's amoral use of military and large-scale technology. Many managers, engineers, and scientists involved in America's publicly funded projects came to distrust the highly rational, planned, and coordinated system of analysis and management developed by McNamara for the purpose of military destruction. Thomas Hughes suggests that the 1960s may be a watershed decade in the history of project management when projects like the ARPANET—which built the computer communications system used by the Internet—began to express the counterculture values of the age. The creators of the ARPANET project preferred a flat management structure and its members were collaborative, meritocratic, and reached decisions by consensus (see Chapter 4 on the adhocracy). They rejected the hierarchy, bureaucracy, and control by experts used on pre-1960s projects like Atlas and Polaris.

The systems model of project management assumes that uncertainties facing a project can be identified at the outset and contingency plans put in place to deal with them should they arise while the project is under way. While this approach may work well on routine and simple projects, it ignores the need for adaptability in truly novel and complex projects. In defence, aerospace, and urban construction projects, for example, a planned and clear sequence of action is not always possible because of their extended duration, too many technological unknowns, and the constantly changing conditions, constraints, and pressures. As most large, complex projects contain both predictable and uncertain elements, a balance has to be found between frozen and flexible project planning, and between orderly routines and innovation during project execution. Sylvain Lenfle and Christoph Loch have recently called for project management to return to its 'lost roots' in the adaptive approach pioneered on the Manhattan, Atlas, and Polaris projects, rather than the orderly, rational systems approach with which they became associated.

In Chapter 4, we consider how the spread of the adaptive project structures in the 1960s and 1970s encouraged management scholars to develop new ways of thinking about organizations.

Chapter 4
Arup's adhocracy
and projects in theory

Ove Arup was one of the leading structural engineers of the 20th century. He worked closely on projects with some the world's greatest architects such as Berthold Lubetkin, Renzo Piano, and Richard Rogers. Influenced by Le Corbusier's celebration of engineering and Walter Gropius' belief in the fusion of art and technology, Arup's vision of a 'Total Design' practice called for architects and engineers to work closely together from the start of a project. His firm, Ove Arup and Partners, established in 1946, embodied this design philosophy.

The Sydney Opera House, the firm's breakthrough project, established a new model of architect and engineer collaborating in project teams to innovate and solve challenging problems. With its dramatic roof, the Sydney Opera House was an engineering project of unprecedented complexity. Based on some evocative sketches, the original design was created by the Danish architect Jørn Utzon, without engineering consultation (Figure 6). Arup forged a close partnership with Utzon to find a way of turning his idea into reality. Arup's engineers made pioneering use of computers to model the roof structure and design a building made of large, prefabricated concrete shells.

Although Ove Arup died in 1988, his collaborative problem-solving approach is evident in Arup's current projects. Today Arup is a

6. An early sketch of the Sydney Opera House, 1956–7.

global professional service organization headquartered in London employing nearly 13,000 staff in about 90 offices in 37 countries. Specialists in engineering, architecture, design, planning, project management, economics, and other disciplines work on as many as 10,000 projects at any particular time. Each project addresses a client's requirement for a system, building, infrastructure, or an entire city. Clients change their minds, building requirements alter, regulations change, and political circumstances are often in flux. All of these constantly changing situations, uncertainties, and overlapping activities have to be addressed by multidisciplinary groups of experts within and outside Arup.

From the Sydney Opera House to Centre Pompidou in Paris and the UK's Channel Tunnel Rail Link, Arup has been involved in challenging projects which have opened up new markets for the firm. One of Arup's more recent high-profile projects was a pioneering urban design completed in 2008 for a Chinese 'eco-city', called Dongtan, situated on Chongming Island near Shanghai. With a proposed population of 500,000 by 2050, Dongtan aimed to be the world's first purpose-built ecologically sustainable city and as close to zero-carbon as possible, with efficient water, renewable energy and recycling systems, and city vehicles that produce no carbon or particulate emissions (Figure 7). Arup's Dongtan contract with the Shanghai Industrial Investment Corporation was followed by a deal signed in London in the

7. Arup's eco-city vision of Dongtan East Village and East Lake.

presence of Hu Jintao, China's president, and Tony Blair, Britain's prime minister, for the two companies to cooperate on future eco-city projects.

Bringing together people with expertise in architecture, urban design, project management, environmental consulting, and economics, a small team of highly motivated and experienced individuals, including Roger Wood, Alejandro Gutierrez, Shanfeng Dong, and others, was formed to lead the Dongtan project and develop the masterplan design. Arup's co-located Dongtan project team was based in the client's Shanghai head office. The project grew into a large multidisciplinary and multicultural organization of around 150 staff at peak, including people born in twenty different countries and located in twelve offices around the world. It was eventually established as part of a separate new business unit, Integrated Urbanism, led by Peter Head. The new unit comprised thirty specialist teams, each consisting of three or four people borrowed from Arup's disciplines, to deal with the cross-cutting social, economic, environmental, and physical components of an eco-city.

Using Arup's matrix approach, the specialist teams (for example, water, waste, logistics, and the new discipline of cultural planning) collaborated with others in multidisciplinary groups to enable quick resolution to design matters. This approach stimulated innovation, but it also brought its own creative tensions as the Dongtan team was under intense pressure to deliver the design quickly to meet the changing priorities and needs of a demanding client. With few precedents to learn from, a radically new sustainable urban design and process for managing a fast-paced project had to be created almost from scratch. As one of Arup's senior designers noted in an interview, 'we did what normally takes four years in one year'. Arup had to address the poorly understood preferences of future residents, businesses, government bodies, and other stakeholders and achieve challenging targets for sustainable performance. A new digital modelling tool, the Integrated Resource Model, was created to identify the numerous interdependencies among multiple technological and organizational components of an integrated urban system.

Although Dongtan was called a 'City of Dreams' by *The Economist* and ultimately never built as a zero-carbon development, the project did provide Arup with an experience base in eco-city design and a credible reputation in this growing market. Members of the Dongtan team were redeployed to win and execute a number of eco-city design projects. The knowledge gained during this significant but unrealized project was codified and new digital planning and project management processes were developed and applied on subsequent projects in China and around the world.

In the late 1960s, when Arup was designing the Sydney Opera House and other firms were discovering adaptable ways of organizing project work, the founders of PMI, APM, and other professional bodies formulated and promoted guidelines, processes, and bodies of knowledge that have become standard in the discipline of project management (Chapter 3). Perhaps inspired by industrial society's view that there is a single best way of organizing, they developed an optimized, fixed, and simple model to execute projects as planned in predictable and carefully controlled phases. This approach assumes that project management can be decoupled from changes in the environment. It works well when technologies and markets are reasonably well understood and plans can be established to deal with known and predictable conditions when the project is under way. As the Arup case illustrates, however, a standardized approach is less well equipped for uncertain, changing, and complex projects.

In the rest of this chapter, we discuss some of the theoretical insights and perspectives introduced by organizational scholars to help us think about projects as a flexible and adaptive structure in a dynamically changing environment.

Organization theory and the adhocracy

While projects became widely used in the defence industries in the 1950s, it was not until the mid-1960s that researchers first noticed this new species of temporary and adaptive organization. About the same time, an influential group of scholars began to challenge the prevailing view that there is one best way of organizing suitable for all environments. In what became known as 'contingency theory', they argued that the design of a successful organization—including a project-based one—reflects the complexity, uncertainty, and rate of change in the technology and market environment.

Traditional industrial organizations have 'mechanistic' structures to perform standardized operations (e.g. mass produced consumer goods and services) and solve routine problems in a relatively stable environment with a greater reliance on predictable tasks broken down into functional specialisms. Individuals occupy sharply defined slots in a division of labour and fit into a vertical hierarchy, with communication running from the boss at the top down to the lowliest worker. In a departure from this rigidity and permanence, Tom Burns and G. M. Stalker argued that organizations adapted to unstable and changing environments have 'organic' structures. This fluid form of organization depends on people communicating horizontally—or 'sideways'—with colleagues as peers working on novel and complex problems that require the continuous adjustment and redefinition of tasks.

Warren Bennis coined the term 'organic-adaptive' to describe the growth in ad hoc project groups combining diverse functional specialists—such as finance, engineering, and marketing—in temporary, problem-solving organizations, which he believed were better equipped to survive in an increasingly turbulent environment. Whereas the mechanistic organizations are designed to survive and grow indefinitely, a project is a temporary organization: it terminates at a specified end state or when a goal has been accomplished. Diversely skilled people who are often unfamiliar with each other's skills are brought together to work on interdependent tasks to achieve a specific goal in a defined period of time. Joan Woodward suggested that organizations drawn to organic structures include those that frequently change their products and 'unit producers' of unique, one-off, or heavily customized products in projects for clients in industries as diverse as aerospace, defence, shipbuilding, music recording, and film making.

James Thompson introduced some of the concepts we use to understand how organizations coordinate interdependent tasks in projects. In 'pooled interdependency', work is broken down into simple tasks performed separately by a functional department with little or no input from others. Standardized rules and procedures are required to ensure that tasks performed in isolation by one functional department provide a discrete contribution without impairing the activities of another department.

In 'sequential interdependency', there is a direct serial relationship between project tasks: the outputs produced in one phase of a project (information, materials, and components) become inputs necessary for the performance of the next phase. Tasks performed sequentially are planned and scheduled in carefully defined phases to achieve a defined project goal. As we saw in Chapter 3, this occurs in serial development when a functional group (e.g. engineering) in a project finishes its task before handing the finished job to the next group (e.g. manufacturing). In the traditional 'waterfall model' of project management, sequential phases of a project are separated from each other by strict exit and entry criteria. Downstream phases cannot start until earlier ones have fulfilled certain conditions.

In 'reciprocal interdependency', each task is penetrated by the other and tasks must be reciprocally adjusted to match changes to other tasks. This is illustrated by the concurrent development of weapons systems in dedicated project organizations (Chapter 3). Design specifications were an input for the production of a missile (technical specifications) and the production of a missile system was an input for the design (the performance requirements of assembly, testing, and launching facilities). Dealing with reciprocal interdependencies requires back-and-forth communication and coordination by the 'mutual adjustment' of tasks as new information becomes available about the project's goal, technology, and market environment.

Projects can be prioritized according to the degree of task interdependency and the coordination required to deal with them. Many projects have pooled, some have pooled and sequential, and the most complex and uncertain have pooled, sequential, and reciprocal interdependencies. In a stable and predictable environment, projects can be defined, planned, and scheduled in advance (using processes identified by the PMI) to deal with pooled and sequential interdependencies. In unstable and rapidly changing conditions—NASA's zone of uncertainty (Chapter 3)—coordination by mutual adjustment is required to address unforeseen interactions, respond to feedback from experience, and adapt in real time to changes in circumstances and goals.

Paul Lawrence and Jay Lorsch help us understand that members of multiple parties in a project organization have to be combined, or 'integrated', to reach agreement on how to respond to the demands of the environment. When projects are complex and interdependent, various liaison positions, or 'linking pins', are needed to coordinate work laterally and obtain cooperation within and between project teams and functional units. As an integrator, a project manager acts in a liaison, persuasion, and negotiation capacity, resolving conflicts that arise when people with specialized knowledge and different interests, viewpoints, and practices are brought together and expected to work in smoothly functioning cross-functional and multiparty projects. Jay Galbraith describes how American aerospace firms created the matrix structure

(Chapter 3) as a dual-reporting integration mechanism to establish a balance of power between functional and project lines of authority. An integrator understands the orientations of differing or competing internal groups and is able to influence external organizations and people with the authority and power to support or curtail a project—a role performed so well by Bernard Schriever on the Atlas Project.

Members of organically structured projects teams are often physically co-located—working together in the same office throughout a project—to integrate multiple participants and address reciprocal interdependency, as we found in the Atlas Project. In his book on R&D projects, Thomas J. Allen suggested that even the smallest degree of dispersion, such as locating people on different floors of the same building, can undermine the intense interaction and cooperation required in project teams. Close proximity and the regular physical presence of co-workers helps to foster more frequent communication, build trust, forge closer interpersonal relationships and informal interactions, and strengthen social ties among team members. There are often a few key individuals in project teams to whom others frequently turn for information. These 'technological gatekeepers' as Allen called them are skilled in translating and articulating diverse functional languages and communicating technical information across organizational boundaries.

In the 1970s, insights and concepts from contingency theory were used to identify the key characteristics of the project organization. In his book *The Structuring of Organizations* (1979), Henry Mintzberg borrowed the word 'adhocracy' from Alvin Toffler (Chapter 1) to identify the project as a new form of organization which combines people with diverse expertise in transient project teams working to solve complex, ill-structured problems and dissolves when the task is accomplished. This organization is based on an organic structure, unit production, problem-solving innovation, coordination by face-to-face mutual adjustment, and horizontal integration mechanisms. Boundaries between disciplines become increasingly blurred as information flows horizontally and freely between people in cross-functional teams. The selection of team members tends to be based on a person's expertise and their ability to work collaboratively, rather than their position or rank in the managerial hierarchy. The knowledge and experience assembled in the team is the base for creating innovation and continuously developing new knowledge.

Adhocracies can be temporary or permanent. In a temporary adhocracy, a standalone organization is assembled to undertake a project and disbands on completion, such as a single film production, an election campaign for a single candidate, an Olympic body established to build and host a single Games, and the joint venture organization established to coordinate a megaproject such as Boston's Central/Artery Tunnel.

In a permanent adhocracy, multiple projects are embedded in two types of parent organizations. One type—the 'operating adhocracy'—undertakes projects for external clients, such as an architectural practice, engineering consultancy, construction contractor, film producer, or advertising agency. An operating adhocracy never really stabilizes. Strategies emerge and evolve in response to the needs of clients—like Arup's Dongtan project—and the adhocracy adapts continuously as projects change and new ones come along, living from one project to the next and disappearing when it can find no more. To ensure a steady and balanced stream of incoming projects, managers of an operating adhocracy spend a great deal of time developing relationships with potential customers and negotiating contracts with them.

Another type of permanent entity—the 'administrative adhocracy'—undertakes projects only to serve itself, not external clients. Operational tasks are cut off from the rest of the parent organization, so that the administrative core is organized in project teams and free to focus on problem-solving and innovation. For example, much of the R&D and overall systems integration work on the Apollo programme was conducted in-house by NASA, but the development of components and subsystems and provision of services and expertise was contracted out to a network of external suppliers.

New thinking about project organizing

The adaptive and innovative capacity of Mintzberg's adhocracy depends on smoothly functioning project teams, which vary in composition, size, and scope. Some projects are undertaken by people who already know each other in small in-house project teams. Others are composed of many individuals from around the world with different backgrounds and perspectives, as illustrated by Arup's Dongtan project. Many large projects are broken down into smaller subprojects, each undertaken by a separate multiparty team. The construction in London of the new Heathrow Terminal 5, for example, was organized as a programme divided into 16 major projects and 147 subprojects, with the smallest valued at £1 million, to large projects, such as the £300 million Heathrow Express underground railway station. Each subproject was undertaken by a multiparty integrated project team comprising members from the client and contractor organizations (Chapter 6).

Recent research suggests that the classic studies placed too much emphasis on the organic-adaptive nature of project teams. Project teams often combine organic and mechanistic, and co-located and dispersed elements. Some teams have the flexibility required to cope with dynamically changing environments, while others are relatively stable structures.

In a study of product development projects undertaken by American, European, and Asian computer firms, Kathleen Eisenhardt and Behnam Tabrizi identified two contrasting models for accelerating the pace of development. A 'compression' strategy is designed to simplify and compress the time taken to complete sequential steps in a well-known and clearly defined process. An 'experiential' strategy of adaptation relies on improvisation, flexibility, and trial-and-error learning to deal with an uncertain and fast-changing process. The study found that successful new product development calls for a subtle blend of these mechanistic and organic processes. Multifunctional teams led by powerful project leaders use planned milestones to compress time and set the pace, but also depend on improvisation and real-time learning through design iterations and testing when conditions change unexpectedly.

Using insights from contingency theory, Amy Edmondson distinguishes between stable and flexible project teams. Stable project teams bring people together with the right combination of skills and experience and have time to build trust to accomplish simple and predictable tasks for existing customers and well-understood situations. Membership is clearly defined: each person or group knows which task to perform and no one has to cross disciplinary boundaries, deal with unexpected events, or do entirely new types of work.

Flexible project teams, by contrast, are required in complex, uncertain, and fast-changing situations, such as product design, research, rescue operations, and strategy development. New groupings of people and organizations—including highly experienced as well as novice team members—are assembled to tackle unique, one-off problems, time and time again. People from different disciplines and other external specialists work in multiple, co-located teams that vary in duration, have constantly shifting membership, and pursue moving targets. Because work is temporary and cuts across functional, geographical, and organizational boundaries, members of a project team have little time to build trust and grow accustomed to each other's working styles, strengths, and weaknesses. There is a need to sort tasks by level of interdependence, but also for coordination by mutual adjustment to keep plans flexible. Project teams learn and execute at the same time, pace their activities to meet deadlines in a limited period of time, and respond to problems and innovative opportunities when they arise.

In a process Edmondson calls 'teaming', flexible teams depend on leaders who can emphasize purpose, build psychological safety, tolerate the inevitable failures that come with experimentation, and embrace conflict and miscommunication that arise when shifting and diverse groups of people with different values and competing priorities start working together. Arup's project to design and build the Water Cube aquatics centre for the Beijing 2008 Olympics illustrates how teaming works. This complex task could not be accomplished by traditional project management planning and efforts to divide up tasks into sequential phases. The team brought together people from twenty disciplines in four countries and external specialists working in collaborative groupings that were formed and dissolved in response to many unforeseen problems that were identified and resolved as the work progressed.

An increasing number of firms are organizing global projects over distance, using digital communications (e.g. email, voice, mobile, and web-based services) and periodic face-to-face meetings to coordinate tasks and forge collaboration amongst team members (Chapter 5). Firms like IBM, General Electric, and SAP have created competency centres to bring together people with relevant expertise from multiple locations to perform specific tasks in spatially dispersed project teams. Members of dispersed teams are geographically spread across cities, countries, and continents, come from different disciplinary backgrounds, speak different languages, and live in different countries with different values, interests, and beliefs.

Collaborating in spatially dispersed teams can be more difficult than in a co-located office. Physical distance can be a hindrance to togetherness and familiarity, resulting in reduced trust, an inability to find a common ground, and difficulties in coordination and cooperation. Members of a dispersed project—or 'virtual' team—may have to adapt work patterns and reorganize schedules to accommodate differences in time zones. If team members are regularly unavailable to discuss problems or clarify how tasks have to be adjusted to resolve them, situations easily addressed in face-to-face meetings can unravel, resulting in frustration, disagreement, and conflict.

In some global industries, such as software development, spatially distributed teams have been known to outperform teams that are co-located. Teams in the same building often underestimate the barriers to collaboration, such as the inconvenience of having to climb a flight of stairs to meet a co-worker. By contrast, software teams that are spread around the world are often more aware of difficulties involved in collaborating and make extra efforts to improve communication and interaction. Periodic face-to-face group meetings help to build team cohesion, develop a shared understanding of the task at hand, and support informal communication. Informal interactions, such as 'going out for a beer with team members', help to establish the common ground and 'rules of the road' before starting a virtual collaboration.

Contingent dimensions of projects

Building on contingency arguments, many scholars now recognize that projects differ greatly in their degree of uncertainty, complexity, and urgency and suggest that distinctive forms of organization, process, and managerial approach are required to manage each of these dimensions. Arthur Stinchcombe's and Carol Heimer's in-depth study of North Sea oil and gas projects was one of the first attempts at applying contingency theory to large-scale projects. They recognized that the highly uncertain and unexpected situations frequently encountered in one-off projects have to be resolved by innovative and adaptive processes, but emphasized that projects incorporate many features we associate with permanent, mechanistic, and stable structures. Contracts between multiple parties in projects incorporate some of the functions managerial hierarchies are set up to achieve, such as incentives and controls to address uncertain and changing conditions.

Uncertainty refers to the state of information about the project's goal, task, and environment, which is often poorly understood and inadequate particularly at the start, as we saw in the Manhattan Project. Uncertainties can be foreseeable and unforeseeable, each of which requires a different project management approach.

A 'foreseen uncertainty' is an event or risk—or 'known unknown'—that can be identified while planning for a project. Risk management is the technique used to identify, evaluate, and control uncertainties that might be avoided or mitigated. Risk registers (i.e. a record of identified risks) are completed before executing a project to identify the technical events (e.g. test or interface problems), partner selection, customer requirements (changes in scope), and other risks. Handling risks means simply accepting them as an unavoidable nuisance or taking preventive action to avoid them, including contingency plans (with reserve funding and time buffers) with instructions for dealing with them if and when they occur.

An 'unforeseen uncertainty' refers to an event, impact, or unanticipated interaction that cannot be identified at the start. Sometimes called 'unknown unknowns', this type of uncertainty occurs frequently in any project that develops new technology, opens up a new or partially understood market, or has to tackle an unanticipated crisis or disaster. Traditional risk management tools are unable to cope with breakthrough projects or projects undertaken in fast-paced competitive environments where unforeseen uncertainty is unavoidable or seen as a risk worth taking, such as Arup's futuristic eco-city design for Dongtan.

Projects have to cope with a variety of economic, institutional, and ecological uncertainties classified by their source and impact. Technological and market uncertainties are singled out by Aaron Shenhar and Dov Dvir as the most widespread, persistent, and challenging unpredictable and unknown factors affecting the goal and tasks undertaken in projects. There are four types of technological uncertainty—low-tech, medium-tech, hi-tech, and super-high-tech projects. Each is associated with how much new technology is incorporated into the final product and the process used to produce it (see Chapter 5 on the use of digital technology to develop the Boeing 777 aeroplane). Projects incorporating significant amounts of new technology (e.g. defence, computer, and aerospace projects) require greater interaction among team members, numerous design cycles, iterative learning, and prototyping. The more new technology employed or developed on a project, the greater the likelihood of cost, time, and quality overruns, and risk of not achieving planned performance objectives.

Market novelty is the uncertainty about the goal or outcome a project is set up to achieve. It refers to the extent to which buyers are familiar with the product and its potential uses and able to articulate their requirements for new or improved products. For example, the fashions and tastes of air travellers—such as demand for low-budget airlines or long-haul flights—are reflected in the airlines' requirements for new planes which are designed and produced by Boeing and Airbus. Building on classification of innovation discussed at length in Chapter 5, Shenhar and Dvir distinguish between derivative, platform, and breakthrough projects. The newer the product, the more difficult it is to identify what customers need and define their requirements during the design stage of a project.

In projects established to develop a major advance in technology or create a new market, traditional risk management techniques would encourage the team to 'get back to the plan', when in practice they need to learn new things, adjust tasks, and change direction. Rather than attempting to tackle unexpected situations by more rigorous application of planning and risk management, Christoph Loch and his co-authors recommend that teams should rely on a combination of 'flexibility and learning'. When too many unknowns exist to allow accurate forecasts of risks, project goals, formal plans, scheduled tasks, and ongoing processes have to be adjusted as new information becomes available and the organization learns more about the project and how it interacts with the environment. As shown in the Manhattan and Atlas projects (Chapter 3), unforeseen uncertainties can be reduced by engaging in multiple and parallel trials to gather valuable information before selecting among alternatives. The costs of repeated tests and experiments may be less than the cost of deciding on a single technology at the outset, which subsequently faces major difficulties not originally envisaged or which becomes outdated when the product is launched.

Flexibility and learning may help managers distinguish between different types of projects according to the degree of uncertainty and adjust their management approach to deal with it. As Sylvain Lenfle and Christoph Loch show in their insightful study of the Manhattan Project, the need for such adaptive processes is apparent not just for different types of projects, but also within large, complex projects. A strategy of targeted flexibility can be used to break down large projects into distinct subprojects to address different pieces of uncertainty. Specific structures, processes, and risk management techniques are required to cope with foreseeable (contingency planning and instructions) and unforeseeable pieces of uncertainty (parallel trials and iterative learning). The London 2012 Olympics project, for example, employed a variety of contracts to target the uncertainty associated with the construction of different venues. Collaborative risk-sharing contracts were relied upon to deal with more uncertain projects (e.g. the distinctive Zaha Hadid designed Aquatics Centre), whereas fixed-price contracts were used for routine and predictable ones (e.g. temporary venues comprising standardized and reusable components).

The structure of a project organization reflects the complexity of the product or system it produces, as we saw in the Atlas Project. The product or outcome of each project involves numerous interconnected parts, components, subsystems, and entire systems, including physical artefacts (e.g. hardware and software) and intangible services (e.g. logistics, maintenance, and operations). Studies have distinguished between projects based on their increasing degree of complexity, ranging from materials, components, and product assemblies to more complex platforms, systems, and 'system of systems' projects. Increasing complexity calls for more elaborate forms of organization and processes (such as a modular design strategy) to cope with the challenge of integrating multiple components, managing interfaces between subprojects, and dealing with reciprocal interdependency (Box 6).

In their three-part classification of project complexity, Shenhar and Dvir suggest that complexity affects interdependencies among tasks and shapes the organization required to manage each project. A relatively simple assembly project is a single component, service, or product with a complex assembly (e.g. a radio base station in a mobile communications network) which is often conducted in-house by a small product development team. A system project consists of components and subsystems, often part of a platform, with multiple functions that together meet a specific operational requirement, such as the development of a new computer, car, or aeroplane. Managed by a large prime contractor with in-house systems integration capabilities (Chapter 3), a central project or programme office is often established to coordinate the technical efforts of the network of in-house functional groups and external suppliers involved in each system project. The most complex array—or system of systems—project consists of a large collection of systems, each serving their own

Box 6 Modularity and systems integration

Electronics-based components produced for the Atlas Project (Chapter 3) often came in black metal boxes with clearly defined interfaces so that it was not necessary to open the 'black box' when assembling the system. Inspired by a similar design strategy, many complex projects in construction, oil and gas, aerospace, and nuclear power plants are composed of modular components with standardized interfaces to simplify the process of construction and integration. Modular components can be produced with greater precision and more cheaply in offsite factories, tested in trial runs, and then assembled onsite like a model kit. For example, 'The Shard', London's 310-metre building designed by Renzo Piano, used prefabricated and pre-assembled modular components and steel structures, which were tested off site prior to their installation on a congested site above the London Bridge railway station.

Modular components are designed to be mixed and matched—rather like Lego bricks—with minimal uncertainty and coordinated via arm's-length market transactions without relying on the conscious intervention of a systems integrator. The seamless inter-firm project coordination promised by modularity is, however, rarely achieved in practice. In their studies of complex projects, Stefano Brusoni and Andrea Prencipe found that firms with capabilities in systems integration are required to oversee the overall design and development of each individual module, accommodate numerous component interactions and adjustments, and tighten the links amongst suppliers of components.

specific purpose, that work together to achieve a common goal, such as a new airport, urban development, or nationwide mobile network. A large systems integrator organization—such as a standalone client organization or joint venture delivery partner—is usually established to deal with financial, legal, and political issues and coordinate and schedule multiple contractors within a large programme.

Projects can be classified according to their urgency, depending on how much time there is available to complete the task and what happens if the time goals are not met. The pace and sequencing of tasks can be driven by chronological time—calendar and clock time—including contracts and time-lines to demarcate and coordinate who does what and when in a project. Pace can be driven by events—predefined deadlines and milestones—to maintain a sense of urgency and focus attention on keeping within the time allocated to complete the project. Predefined milestones establish specific dates when certain tasks should be accomplished or completed more rapidly before moving to the next stage, such as the completion of a design freeze in a product development project. Lars Lindkvist and his co-authors found that the project team responsible for introducing Ericsson's first mobile communications system in Japan had to accept an incredibly tight deadline. In what was considered an 'impossible task', the team dramatically shortened the time taken to deliver the project after they shifted from a sequential to a new 'fountain model' of concurrent development driven by a very clear goal (delivering a fully operational system by 1 April 1994), unambiguous deadlines, and frequent milestones.

In their four-part classification of project pace, Shenhar and Dvir emphasize that the more urgent the project, the greater the need for autonomy, rapid decision making, and senior management involvement. Regular projects—such as many public construction works or organizational change programmes—are endeavours where some time delay may be tolerated. Fast-competitive projects found in most industries and profit-driven organizations, by contrast, have to respond rapidly to market opportunities, build new lines of business, and create a strategic advantage. Time-critical projects are those that are constrained by a window of opportunity (e.g. buildings for the Millennium celebrations) or must be completed by a specified date (e.g. major events in the sporting calendar such as the Olympic Games or FIFA World Cup). Missing the deadline results in project failure. Blitz projects are formed to deal with the most urgent problems—natural disasters, emergencies, or crisis situations—as quickly as possible, such as the successful rescue of the 33 Chilean miners trapped 700 metres underground for 69 days in 2010. They require more autonomy and resources than any other project to deal with emergent and on-the-spot situations that must be handled almost instantaneously and move rapidly and flexibly to save lives, protect property, and restore order to chaotic situations.

In recent years, several influential scholars have attempted to develop conceptual frameworks that address the contingent dimensions of projects. In their book *Managing the Unknown* (2006), Christoph Loch, Arnoud DeMeyer, and Michael Pich identify different approaches for managing projects in technology and market environments ranging from simple and predictable to novel and unknown. A contingency theory of project management appears in research articles by Shenhar and Dvir and is brought together in their book *Reinventing Project Management* (2007). They argue that there is no one-size-fits-all structure or process suitable for all projects. Some projects are simple and predictable, while many are complex, uncertain, and strongly shaped by the dynamics of the environment.

In Chapter 5 we consider how project management was transformed in the 1980s and 1990s to manage innovation in increasingly competitive global markets.

Chapter 5
Lean, heavy, and disruptive projects

The world market for cars was dominated during most of the 20th century by a handful of giant mass production enterprises—Ford, General Motors, and Chrysler in the United States and Volkswagen, Renault, Fiat, BMW, Daimler-Benz, and a few others in Europe. By the 1980s, however, the Western monopoly of the global automotive industry was under threat. Japanese car manufacturers Honda and Toyota had discovered a way of developing and producing an enormous variety of new models in high volume at less expense and more rapidly than their Western counterparts. In a study of product development projects in the world motor industry undertaken between 1983 and 1987, Kim Clark and Takahiro Fujimoto found that a new Japanese car required on average 1.7 million engineering hours and 46 months from first design to customer delivery, whereas it took Western producers 3 million engineering hours and 60 months. Japan's producers were 'lean' because each new product development project was developed with less than half the number of people and in nearly half the time.

Lean product development

In the 1980s all car manufacturers, Japanese and Western, used some form of matrix to organize their product development projects (Chapter 3). Experts from different functional units—marketing, engineering (power train, body chassis, and process), and manufacturing—had to collaborate intensively in projects to develop a new car. Each firm had a range of different models, components, and factories that had to be shared. When a new product was developed, the division leading the endeavour had to interact with other divisions and component suppliers that manufactured the shared parts. In practice, however, a Japanese matrix bore little or no resemblance to a Western one. In *The Machine that Changed the World* (1990)—the book that introduced the idea of lean production—James Womack, Daniel Jones, and Daniel Roos distinguished between the traditional Western and revolutionary new Japanese approach to product development.

The 'mass production' development approach used by Western producers is illustrated by General Motors in the 1980s. In a sequential development process (Chapter 4), the project was 'handed over the wall' from one functional department to the next during its life and worked upon by different and fragmented groups along the way. The parties involved had to reach thousands of decisions on specifications, performance, and appearance including the target market, price, most appealing features, and physical dimensions of the car. Engineers then had to work out precise specifications for each part and which parts could be obtained from other GM products. Hirotaka Takeuchi and Ikujiro Nonaka likened this approach to the passing of the baton in a relay race. Similar to NASA's 'phased program planning' (Chapter 3), the product moves through highly structured phases: concept development, feasibility testing, product design, development, pilot, production, and product launch.

GM appointed a programme manager to lead and coordinate members of the project team on short-term loan from functional departments. In a weak position to champion the project within the firm, GM's programme managers did not have the authority needed to insist that their orders were obeyed. Acting more like coordinators than managers, they were often reluctant to confront conflicts and struggled to convince members and functional groups to cooperate. When they urged engineering departments and others to commit to design decisions or move faster, they were met with promises rather than action. The communication required to solve problems was often poor because the design process was sequential and dispersed, rather than being co-located at team headquarters. The number of people involved in design decisions was small at the start, growing to a peak as the project proceeded to product launch, when far too many new people were brought in to solve problems that should have been addressed at the outset.

The 'lean' approach was created by Honda and Toyota to develop a wider range of products faster and with fewer errors than their Western counterparts. Development work was subdivided to address the demands of different geographical markets around the world. Once the product plan and specifications were set, dedicated members of the project team worked rapidly with no interruptions to achieve the overall goal, collaborating with the functional departments when necessary.

A project leader—Honda's Large Project Leader or Toyota's '*shusa*'—was appointed to head the development of each new model, with the authority to acquire resources and manage, rather than simply coordinate, the development process. Although Japanese producers also used a matrix structure, people were borrowed from the functional departments and transferred for the life of each project. They worked in a tightly knit team—with far fewer staff than Western projects—under the control of the 'heavyweight project manager' (see 'Team structures and leaders'). A collaborative problem-solving approach was fostered by the continuity of team membership and shared experience developed while working together on past projects. Communication among members and different disciplines was greatest at the start of the design process when all the relevant expertise was brought together. The heavyweight project manager's job was to encourage members to confront trade-offs and resolve conflicts over resources. Motivated by the project's guiding vision, individual members signed formal pledges to do what everyone agreed upon as a team.

Japanese firms in other consumer goods industries such as Fuji-Xerox and Canon developed an adaptive 'overlay' approach for developing new products in overlapping (or concurrent) phases—adding flexibility to the acceleration in pace provided by lean. Using the overlay approach, teams can absorb new information and engage in an iterative and adaptive process of trial-and-error learning to narrow down the number of alternatives they must consider—similar to the use of concurrency on the Atlas Project (Chapter 3).

Over the past two decades, lean development has spread to many industries experiencing rapid product obsolescence and shorter product life cycles, such as consumer electronics and other fast-paced environments. It has been adopted by unit producers, such as aerospace, construction, and film making (e.g. Pixar), where concurrent product development and cooperative relationships are used to generate new ideas, drive performance, and communicate any desired changes while the project is under way.

Lean development supported by digital technology

By the 1990s, fast, flexible, and lean development processes were increasingly used in conjunction with digital technologies—computer-aided-design (CAD), computer-aided-manufacturing (CAM), and telecommunication systems—to coordinate co-located and dispersed teams involved in the design, production, integration, and testing of new products.

The Boeing 777, for example, was the first commercial aeroplane designed entirely using computers. Originally conceived in 1988, the design of Boeing's new long-range, wide-body, twin-engine aeroplane with fly-by-wire computer controls was decided upon in March 1990. After a period of development and extensive testing, the first 777 aeroplane entered service with United Airlines on 7 June 1995. On Boeing's previous development projects, physical drawings had been thrown over the wall between spatially and organizationally separate design and manufacturing teams. On the 777 project, by contrast, every engineer had access to digital information and three-dimensional designs were often exchanged back and forth online between closely interacting teams. Rather than wait until physical drawings were copied and checked for compatibility, an engineer on the 777 project could use the computer to call up all the parts and identify interferences or 'clashes' when they were fitted together (Box 7).

In his biography of the 777 project, Karl Sabbagh found that in 'the fiercely competitive world of plane-making, it is project management that Boeing hope will give their plane the edge over Airbus and McDonnell Douglas'. The development of the 777 was led by two of Boeing's most powerful and experienced project managers. Alan Mulally, who would later become Chief Executive of Ford, ran the project during the most intense phases of design and manufacture after the previous manager, Phil Conduit, left to become Boeing's Chief Executive. Boeing's 777 digital design technology worked well because it was embedded in a highly collaborative and problem-solving project organization. Under Mulally's leadership, Boeing established an approach called 'Working Together' to encourage engineers to meet face to face, exchange ideas of mutual interest, resolve conflicts, build trust, and develop a shared understanding about what they were trying to create (Figure 8). Boeing also adopted the collaborative 'design-build' project teams pioneered in Japan, so that airline customers and external suppliers were involved in early design decisions.

The availability of digital technologies—CAD, CAM, and network-based broadband communication delivered by web

Box 7 Boeing's 'paperless plane'

Computer-aided design had been used in automotive manufacturing, civil engineering, and architecture as a drawing tool, but never on the scale implemented by Boeing. Two linked computer systems were used to design, assemble, and test a simulation of the 777 aeroplane: Computer-Aided Three dimensional Interactive Application (CATIA) and Electronic Preassembly in the CATIA. CATIA was developed for the aerospace industry by Dassault and in collaboration with IBM. Using this paperless system, engineers could zoom in on one part and zoom out and see how that part fitted in a whole plane composed of four million parts. Boeing's Everett, Washington, factory, the main design location for the 777, was equipped with 2,200 computer terminals connected to IBM mainframe computers. Eventually members of the project had access to over 7,000 workstations dispersed around the world in over seventeen time zones. A dedicated private data network was laid across the Pacific Ocean from Washington to Japan, where the Japanese Aerospace Industry consortium of companies was responsible for designing 20 per cent of the fuselage structure. All the 238 project teams, each comprising up to 40 engineers, had access to computer data. The CAD programme supplied the CAM system with digital data required to produce components of the fuselage. The system provided a complete digital model of the component parts of the 777 which maintenance staff needed when the plane was in service.

browsers and stored in 'the cloud'—over the past two decades coincided with the adoption of lean and more collaborative ways of managing projects. Digital technologies have spread from aerospace to more traditional sectors like construction to assist with the design, construction, integration, as well as the 'virtual' testing of components and systems.

8. The phrase 'Working Together', a management style that contributed to the smooth running of the project, is used as the name of the first Boeing 777.

Frank Gehry, for example, purchased CATIA aerospace software (used on the Boeing 777 project) from IBM in 1991 to design and build the Guggenheim Museum in Bilbao, northern Spain. The building contains gallery spaces for the exhibition of works of internationally recognized contemporary artists. It would have been impossible to design and build such a complex construct without the aid of computers. With its loose arrangement of curved shapes designed to catch the light, the building was constructed with a steel frame to form crumpled shapes, covered in glass, limestone, and titanium-coated tiles that could adapt to the curves of the exterior building. The steel and titanium components were first manufactured and cut to shape with greater precision under factory conditions and then assembled on the site. Based on a detailed and realistic cost estimate before commencing, the project was successfully delivered on time and within budget. Since the museum opened on 18 October 1997, the benefits of this spectacular and awe-inspiring building have far exceeded the costs of the project. It has revived a provincial city by establishing it on the map of global art and architecture, making it a popular place that tourists from around the world want to visit.

The Guggenheim project marked the beginning of Gehry's shift from a traditional to a digitally adapted design practice. Digital tools and processes support collaborative project teams involved in the design and construction of avant-garde, inspirational buildings. A digital model is a 'single source of information' for each project and used as a 'projective argument' for discussions with the client. In a process that Gehry describes as 'fast and adaptable', the digital model is used to explore and test numerous possibilities, experiment with rapid prototyping techniques (where physical models are produced from a 3D digital model), suggest new directions, and continue to make adjustments, if needed, until late stages of a project. Every interdependent part, emerging problem, and changing priority of a project can be seen with a high degree of precision and controlled and managed in real time. Placing architecture at the centre of a collaborative process with clients, engineering consultants, and contractors, Gehry believes that digital tools can help re-establish the role of the architect as 'master builder' in a future (Chapter 1) when all buildings and cities will be designed and built using digital tools, much like the Boeing 777.

Innovation projects

Developing new products and taking an innovative idea from concept to reality is often said to resemble a 'funnel'. Starting with a broad range of inputs, the process gradually refines and selects from among them, and creates a few development projects that converge on a specific product that addresses a stable customer need for an incremental improvement or opens up new and highly uncertain markets for radically new products or services.

In their book *Revolutionizing Product Development* (1992), Steven Wheelwright and Kim Clark developed a classification of development projects according to the degree of novelty in products and processes on a continuum from incremental to radical innovation. There are three types of commercial product development projects. Derivative projects involve incremental innovation and range from cost-reductions to enhancements of existing products and processes. They require fewer development resources than other projects because the customer's requirements are well known and specifications set at an early stage. At the other end of the spectrum, breakthrough projects are based on radical innovation because they introduce entirely novel processes or untried products leading to the creation of entirely new markets and industries. Breakthrough projects require significantly more resources and greater autonomy to decide how to design radically new products and processes. Situated in the middle of the incremental–radical innovation continuum, platform projects develop new products and processes (sharing standardized, modular, and common components) for existing customers and known markets.

Apple provides an example of a company almost exclusively focused on breakthrough innovation. On many projects, Apple's former CEO, Steve Jobs, had a knack of creating wonderfully designed things people were not aware they needed, but then found they could not live without. Apple's transformation into one of the world's most successful firms began with a breakthrough project: the iPod music player, unveiled on 23 October 2001. Apple disrupted the music industry by changing the way people listen to, make, and buy music. Although Apple's design adopted existing MP3 technology, the iPod was a breakthrough because it worked in tandem with iTunes software, allowing users to manage their own music, pictures, video, text, and other features. It created Apple's digital hub for other breakthrough projects, including the iPhone and iPad. Jobs encouraged development teams to focus on novel ideas and was notoriously impatient with those who stuck to the plan and made compromises in order to get the product out on time and on budget. As Isaacson points out in his biography of Apple's CEO, on the iPhone, Apple store, and other projects, Jobs 'pressed the "pause" button as they neared completion and decided to make major revisions'.

Unlike Apple, few companies have serial breakthrough projects in their portfolio. Commercial airliner manufacturers, for example, establish platform projects to launch each new family of products, such as Boeing's models from the 707 to the most recent 787 plane. Between each generation of product, changes occur in both the customer requirements a product must address and the technologies it uses to satisfy these needs. Boeing undertakes derivative projects to provide enhancements and 'stretch design' improvements that represent the series of modifications within a given model. The 767 designers, for example, stretched the design to accommodate the airlines' requests for more seats, making the plane 14 metres (46 feet) longer.

The other two categories of projects are R&D and alliance and partnership projects. R&D projects convert ideas into new products, services, and processes. They create new knowledge of materials, technologies, and services that are eventually incorporated in new commercial development projects. Because the process and outcome of an R&D project is highly uncertain, firms have different expectations about the resources required to support them than for commercial development projects. Alliance and partnership projects are formed with multiple external parties for any type of R&D or derivative, platform, or breakthrough development projects. In recent years, many firms—Xerox, IBM, Intel, Procter & Gamble, and others—have shifted from a closed model of innovation where R&D and product development projects were largely undertaken in-house to an increasingly open model which leverages internal and external sources of ideas to commercialize a new offering.

Portfolio management

A certain amount of slack in an organization is said to advance innovation by providing the time and space needed to experiment with new and uncertain ideas that might not otherwise attract support when resources are scarce. Innovation is costly and creating too much slack can absorb a firm's valuable resources. A portfolio approach provides a top–down, strategic way of managing innovation and allocating scarce resources to families of sequentially related product development projects. Firms use portfolios to evaluate and map a set of projects into different categories based on their novelty, identify how projects are sequenced over time in waves, and compress the time taken to execute them individually and collectively. The most innovative projects—platforms and breakthroughs—require greater resources, redundancy, and slack to cope with longer and more uncertain development cycles. By mapping the project types and identifying gaps in the product development strategy, managers of portfolios can identify which new projects should be added to the mix, when to add them, and when to terminate them. They can also identify the capabilities and develop the skills that individual members, teams, and project leaders need to plan and execute them.

Strategies used to circumvent strict portfolio evaluation criteria include various bottom-up, small-scale projects scattered throughout an organization. Requiring only limited resources, these projects can be undertaken covertly within existing business units and often without senior management ever being aware of them. Under-the-table, unofficial 'bootlegging projects'—sometimes embarked on with the tacit support of senior management—are an important source of innovation and entrepreneurship that may later become officially accepted and absorbed by mainstream product development activities. Today many executives have 'side projects' to experiment with an idea, develop a hobby, learn new skills, or create a start-up business free from the constraints of the mainstream organization. Google, for example, is well known for encouraging its employees to develop side projects as part of their day-to-day jobs. Many businesses—Twitter, Craigslist, Flat Planet, and Groupon—started out as side projects.

Team structures and leaders

Wheelwright and Clark developed a well-known classification of four types of project team structures used for product development and innovation in many industries. In the 'functional team structure', tasks are subdivided at the outset into separate activities performed independently by functional groups. The project moves sequentially, although often not smoothly, from one function to the next. When there is limited overlap and interaction amongst team members, functional groups often develop their own habits, routines, and mindsets and face difficulties forming tightly knit cooperative teams with other groups.

In the 'lightweight team structure', members also reside physically in their functional disciplines, but each group designates a liaison manager as its representative on the project coordinating committee. In this matrix form of organization, the manager is said to be lightweight because he or she has less status in the organization, and key resources and power remain under the control of the functional managers. However, there is now at least one manager who looks across the functions to ensure that members of the team are kept informed about any cross-functional issues and interdependent tasks are performed in a timely manner.

In the 'heavyweight team structure', members borrowed from the functional groups are dedicated and physically co-located with the heavyweight project leader. As the Honda, Toyota, and Boeing examples showed, the project leader is a heavyweight because he or she is a senior manager in the organization, often having more expertise, experience, and status than the functional managers. Physical co-location is preferable to online digital communications because problems that arise in real time are best dealt with directly in face-to-face meetings, rather than having to wait for an episodic meeting to occur or use online communication to initiate cross-functional problem-solving. The core team is responsible for subdividing tasks, scheduling the project, and adjusting tasks when circumstances change. A heavyweight team requires a distinctive style of leadership to galvanize and motivate the team, while championing the basic concept being developed by the project—the role performed by Mulally on the 777 project. The heavyweight project manager is able to understand the needs of the customer and market, speak the language of the different functional groups, coordinate and integrate their work, and identify and resolve any conflicts that inevitably arise when groups with different expertise, behaviour, and priorities are expected to work together.

Faced with unforeseen circumstances or opportunities, the heavyweight team is able to develop new knowledge, reallocate resources, and reconfigure tasks to get the work accomplished in the best possible way. Clark and Fujimoto suggested that this structure is most effective for platform projects. American car producers in the mid-1980s using functional or lightweight team structures employed approximately 1,500 engineers in full-time work over several months, whereas Japanese platform projects with heavyweight managers employed only 250 engineers working full-time for the same period.

In the 'autonomous team structure', people from the various functions are also co-located as an integrated team but now with their own home, often in a separate building, for the duration of the project. The project leader, also a heavyweight, has full control over the resources and people provided by the functional groups and is sole evaluator of the performance of individual team members. Sometimes known as a 'tiger team', an autonomous project has a 'clean sheet of paper': it does not have to follow established policies and can make almost any changes required to accomplish the project goal. Members interact informally by mutual adjustment in organically structured teams. Lockheed Martin, the American aerospace and defence company, pioneered what is known as a 'skunk work' organization during the Cold War. It created this autonomous structure to house the cross-functional capabilities required to develop new high-technology projects, such as the U-2 spy-plane, SR-71 Blackbird, and F-117 Stealth Fighter, at a distance from the firm's mainstream organization and unencumbered by established rules and procedures.

The balancing act

Undertaking projects to serve existing customers or create new markets entails a difficult balancing act. Using the metaphor of a stream, Rosabeth Moss Kanter suggests that an organization can maintain projects—'swim with the stream'—it is already committed to in its mainstream technology and market home base or it can cut a new channel and start a new stream of projects that will be of benefit in the future. Organizations require a certain amount of ambidexterity to know how to exploit their mainstream business, while launching breakthrough projects to explore and open up new market opportunities.

Derivative or platform projects in a firm's mainstream business develop incremental enhancements and new products for existing clients with stable preferences and predictable needs in existing markets. When projects depend on familiar technologies, plans and schedules can be developed before action is taken. Firms have a history and experience base, providing data for predictions about the future, an opportunity for careful planning prior to execution, and the ability to allocate resources to different projects and smooth out activities over the calendar year.

Firms are successful in mainstream markets because they listen to their customers and carefully study market trends before investing in new and improved products. It may seem surprising, for example, but until the 1990s Boeing did not generally seek the advice of the airlines before deciding on a new plane. It would develop the idea of a new plane, design and manufacture it, and then wait for airlines to buy it. Faced with intense competition from Airbus and McDonnell Douglas, changing demand for air travel, and other uncertainties, a new approach was needed. Boeing's 777 project team had to spend time with the airlines to find out what they required in terms of range, size, payload, and economy. Meetings with representatives of the 'Gang of Eight'—United, American, Delta, British Airways, Japan Air Lines, All-Nippon Airways, Qantas, and Cathy Pacific—helped Boeing design the 777.

New sources of revenues must be found when mainstream activities stagnate and decline. But the mainstream is often too slow and bureaucratic to compete in volatile markets or cope with rapid product obsolescence. Past investments in resources and commitments—budgets, schedules, role definitions, and expectations—made to keep mainstream projects flowing also make it difficult for them to change direction. Projects carried out by established R&D departments often fail when it comes to creating 'new to the world' products, which do not satisfy the performance requirements of existing customers, as Eastman Kodak, the camera manufacturer, found when it fatally delayed the switch from film to digital technology, which marked the beginning of the company's eventual demise and the rise of Fujitsu, Canon, and others.

Breakthrough projects initiate new streams of innovation. They imagine new possibilities, create entirely new offerings, and disrupt established industries. Because they have little or no experience base in the new technology and there are no current customers to listen to, forecasts about user requirements are difficult to produce, project schedules are usually unrealistic, and costs are likely to overrun. Action must be taken before plans can be developed and tasks have to be adjusted to deal with technical problems and unforeseen events while the project is under way. Existing knowledge is applied where possible, but new knowledge is required to make sense of poorly understood technologies and unknown customer requirements. As Kanter explains:

> Multiple approaches, flexibility, and speed are required for innovation because of the advance of new ideas through random and often highly intuitive insights and because of the discovery of unanticipated problems. Project teams need to work unencumbered by formal plans, board approval, and other 'bureaucratic delays', that might act as constraints against the change of direction.

Because breakthrough projects compete directly with the mainstream for resources, attention, and loyalty, senior management in the parent organization may become nervous about delegating too much control to the autonomous team and its leader. Too often, there is a risk that an autonomous team goes off on a tangent and creates difficulties for the parent organization. It may become too focused on the priorities of the individual project, rather than the needs of the wider organization (Chapter 6). Keeping breakthrough projects separate poses less of a threat to vested interests and helps to create the new culture, entrepreneurialism, and autonomy required to nurture and develop new ideas without being overly constrained by the dictates of established business fiefdoms or cumbersome bureaucratic procedures.

The autonomy required when launching breakthrough projects is illustrated by the development of the IBM Personal Computer (PC) in 1981. IBM established an autonomous team as an independent cross-functional structure called 'Project Chess' led by Bill Lowe. Located in Boca Raton, Florida, the project was far removed from the firm's headquarters and R&D department. This so-called 'renegade team' had a mandate to do whatever was required to develop the personal computer. At the same time, IBM's mainstream project called Datamaster, which continued with the established policy of producing components in-house, was stuck in its fourth year of development with no end in sight. A willingness to break the rules, including buying in components and software (e.g. the operating system) from external suppliers, enabled Project Chess to develop and bring the PC to market in just one year.

Achieving breakthroughs

The most effective breakthrough project teams—like Project Chess—are structurally independent from the existing organization, but supported by top management and tightly integrated into the wider corporate structure. They share resources with traditional units, but being physically and organizationally separate ensures that the new project's processes, values, and approach are not overwhelmed by bureaucratic procedures. With so much responsibility and power delegated to the breakthrough project team, special integration mechanisms have to be put in place to maintain close contact between the team and parent organization. Senior management needs to retain the ability to guide the project, with a strong executive sponsor acting as a coach and mentor for the heavyweight manager and core team. If the members of the senior management team or other functional heads have concerns or require more information about the progress of the project, these can be communicated through the executive sponsor.

Breakthroughs are difficult to accomplish in well-established industries and those dominated by a few large firms likes cars, aeroplanes, mobile phones, and construction. In the early 1990s, for example, innovation in the car industry involved well-understood technologies and demand for its products was growing continuously. James Womack and his co-authors asked whether car producers were able to pass the 'final test' of applying the lean approach to breakthrough innovation: the creation of navigation and congestion-avoidance systems, autonomous driver-less cars, hydrogen and electric vehicles needed to address society's demands for motor-vehicle technology that does not contribute to rising levels of carbon emissions and the pollution of our cities.

Clayton Christensen identified the electric vehicle as the car industry's potentially disruptive technology and recommended that car manufacturers create a small, independent project organization separated from the mainstream, such as GM's Saturn Division, to nurture and commercialize the new technology. While a few firms started to develop electric cars (GM and Renault-Nissan), most focused on improving their existing products or developing hybrids, such as the Toyota Prius (Box 8).

A start-up from outside the industry—the first in the United States since Chrysler was established in 1925—challenged the mainstream manufacturers by producing the first all-electric car. Tesla Motors was founded by Martin Eberhard and Marc Tarpenning in 2003 and financed by serial entrepreneur Elon Musk who became Tesla's CEO. The Tesla Roadster, the first electric sports car, was introduced in 2008, but it was the Tesla Model S introduced in 2012 which launched the firm as an independent volume producer of electric cars. Powered by a battery pack, guided by an on-board computer with an Internet connection, dependent on downloaded software updates, and supported by a network of charging stations, the Model S is considered the 'automotive equivalent to an iPhone' because it can be plugged in and recharged at night. In a recent biography, Musk explains that the established car producers were reluctant to develop all-electric cars because they 'are so derivative. They want to see it work somewhere else before they will approve the project and move forward.' Tesla had to compete with the core capability of every car manufacturer in the world to achieve Musk's vision. The car that began technological disruption of the industry was developed at rapid pace by a small, autonomous project team of experienced engineers with its own office in a corner of Musk's SpaceX factory to 'add some separation and secrecy to what they

> **Box 8 Disruptive technology**
>
> Clayton Christensen suggests that listening to customers helps firms know which 'sustaining technologies' are required to improve the performance of established products that mainstream customers have traditionally valued. At the end of the 20th century, for example, the automotive industry continued to invest in products that their customers wanted: cars fuelled by petrol engines, providing high performance at low prices. At the time, no car producer was threatened by electric vehicles and few were contemplating moving into this uncertain market. But there are times when 'not listening to customers' is the right strategy. This occurs when entrepreneurs invest in high-risk 'disruptive technologies'—like the electric or self-driving autonomous car—which existing customers may not want and result in worse performance in the near term, but ultimately promise to open up new, growing, and lucrative markets.

were doing'. Led by a 'free-spirited, creative' car designer named Franz von Holzhausen, the Model S team had to deal with Musk's demands for numerous design changes, advanced vehicle technologies developed in-house, and aggressive time schedule for product delivery.

Agile project management

An alternative to lean has emerged incorporating some of its adaptive elements but which is even more strongly focused on real-time learning, improvisation, and iterative development. Originally developed for software projects, the 'agile' methodology offers a radical alternative to the traditional standard waterfall model of project management (Chapter 4) and its emphasis on an early design and specification freeze, a fixed scope, sequential phases of planning and execution, and limited customer interaction. Those advocating an agile approach believe that the traditional reliance on rigid front-end planning processes and formal contracts can result in various 'downstream pathologies' such as a lack of flexibility when conditions change, excessive rework, dissatisfied clients, and an inability to adjust in real time to changing circumstances while a project is under way. As we saw in Chapter 1, for example, Motorola's Iridium project developed the full potential of satellite phone technology, only to find that the rapid expansion of terrestrial mobile communications had largely eliminated the need for it while the project was under way.

Relatively stable environments are amenable to front-end planning and scheduling, whereas a changing and uncertain environment requires agile methods so that planning and replanning is spread out across the development life cycle. Agile is an iterative and incremental 'rolling wave' process designed to facilitate flexibility and responsiveness to abruptly changing technology and market conditions. Agile methods require the minimum use of documentation, continuous design iterations so that the design freeze is delayed until the last responsible moment, frequent customer and stakeholder interaction, and a modified lightweight project team structure. An agile approach shares many of the adaptive, real-time 'teaming' processes discussed in Chapter 4. Adjustments are made 'on the fly' to deal with abruptly changing conditions and plans are altered as new information about customer requirements and technologies becomes available during the execution of a project. Growing evidence suggests that agile contributes to the success of software and IT projects, and may be of value for projects undertaken in hi-tech and more traditional industries.

In Chapter 6, we use examples of some of the infrastructure megaprojects undertaken in London over the past decade to illustrate some of the different ways of organizing projects in the 21st century.

Chapter 6
London's megaproject ecology

The Jubilee Line Extension project of the London Underground—a 10-mile (16-kilometre) tube line with cavernous stations—was built to connect London's West End with the office metropolis at Canary Wharf and south and east areas of the city. This time-critical project was supposed to open as a complete system in time to carry millions of passengers to London's Millennium Dome for the millennium celebrations. Based on a fixed-price contract, it was scheduled for completion in March 1997 at a cost of £2.1 billion (an earlier estimate in 1989 was £900 million). It was designed to incorporate the most advanced radio-based, moving block signalling system technology to allow the trains to run closely together, much faster and more safely. It represented the future of travel in the world's congested cities. Construction of the extension started in December 1993 but difficulties with tunnelling and signalling forced the project to abandon the new signalling technology, delayed the completion date, and significantly raised the final cost. Some contractors submitted low-cost tenders on the expectation that they could recoup the money and earn additional profits by submitting over £500 million of claims for changes to the specification and unexpected problems encountered during construction. To resolve these problems, the London Underground was removed from the management of the project in 1998 and replaced by Bechtel, the American engineering and construction firm. The project eventually cost £3.5 billion and was opened in three stages from May to December 1999.

The Jubilee Line is one of a long list of UK megaprojects in the 1980s, 1990s and early 2000s—the Channel Tunnel, Millennium Dome, Scottish Parliament Building, Swanwick Air Traffic Control, and many others—that were overdue and over budget. In a review of the Jubilee Line project, Bechtel concluded that British clients and contractors were incapable of managing large-scale infrastructure projects.

In the late 1990s, BAA (formerly British Airports Authority)—the owner and operator of major UK airports—was preparing to build the £4.3 billion fifth terminal (T5) for British Airways at London's Heathrow Airport (Figure 9). Richard Rogers won the competition to design T5 in 1989, construction started in July 2002, and the terminal opened in March 2008. Sir John Egan, BAA's Chief

9. Heathrow Terminal 5 during construction.

Executive in the 1990s, was aware of the UK construction industry's poor track record in delivering projects and concerned that any significant cost overrun on T5 'could bankrupt the company'. BAA decided to examine every major UK construction project over the previous decade and every international airport that had opened during the previous fifteen years (e.g. Denver and Charles de Gaulle) to find out why megaprojects so often failed.

The answer was surprisingly simple. Clients assumed that future conditions could be foreseen in low-cost bids and accounted for in a fixed-price contract that transferred all risks to the contractor and allowed no room for changes in circumstances (see NASA's view of fixed-price contracts in Chapter 3). When problems arose, there was no collaborative mechanism to resolve them. Disputes between client and contractor frequently ended up in court, delaying the project. BAA knew from its own experience with a fixed-price contract in the mid-1990s—the delayed Heathrow Express railway from the airport to Paddington station—that the risk of delivering a project could not be contracted out to a construction company. If T5 was delivered using the traditional model, BAA estimated that the project would be £1 billion over budget, a year late, and result in six deaths during construction. BAA's insight was that in complex and uncertain projects the client ultimately always bears the risks when things go wrong and it concluded that a radically new 'project delivery model' (the contractual and organizational relationship between client and contractors) was required for T5.

The T5 project was established as an autonomous structure led by a heavyweight team of managers with experience gained in other industries (e.g. automotive, nuclear power, and aerospace) and other complex projects (e.g. GSK's UK research facility and Hong Kong International Airport). This core team 'changed the rules of the game' by creating a new flexible contract called the 'T5 Agreement' based on two principles: the client would bear the risks involved in constructing T5 and work collaboratively with contractors in co-located integrated project teams. Contractors had their costs reimbursed and were incentivized to innovate and improve performance by bonuses for doing better than previously agreed 'target costs' and completion dates. Any profits earned were shared among team members. In contrast to the traditional delivery model, the T5 process was flexible and adaptive to deal with unforeseen events and embrace opportunities to innovate that could not be anticipated at the start:

> Conventional project logic seeks to predefine all requirements and banish change once the project has started. Yet flexibility and adaptability are key objectives for T5. Conventional processes and solutions are therefore not tenable. It will require flexibility of approach: flexibility of solutions; latest responsible decision making.
>
> (*T5 Delivery Handbook*, 1999)

Despite the disrupted opening (Chapter 1), the T5 project was delivered on time and within budget. One year after opening, T5 was voted the world's best airport terminal by passengers. It has radically transformed how megaprojects in the UK are delivered and started an industry-wide narrative about the need for flexibility, collaboration, and innovation. Individuals, teams, and organizations working on T5 carried many of the new ideas and innovative practices with them when they went to work on other megaprojects in London, such as the construction of the £6.8 billion London 2012 Olympics venues and infrastructure, the £14.8 billion Crossrail urban railway system traversing east–west across London, and the £4.2 billion Thames Tideway Tunnel scheme to replace London's ageing Victorian sewer system (Box 9).

As this brief introduction to London's megaprojects illustrates, it is important to understand the context within which projects are initiated and unfold over time. It raises many questions that cannot be answered by project management's traditional preoccupation

Box 9 Inside the world of a megaproject

London's Crossrail project illustrates what it's like to work on one of these massive endeavours. The project is constructing a new railway—the Elizabeth Line—from Reading and Heathrow in the west via 21 km of twin-bore tunnels under central London to Shenfield and Abbey Wood in the east, including ten new and thirty upgraded stations. Many of Crossrail's tunnels (Figure 10) have been excavated and constructed close to existing tube lines. At its closest point, one of Crossrail's tunnels is only 37 cm (15 inches) from the Northern Line tunnel.

One station is underneath the junction between Oxford Street (Europe's busiest shopping street) and Charing Cross Road where a small army of construction workers, electricians, engineers, and project managers have been working to complete the £1 billion transformation of Tottenham Court Road Station. The station and two ticket halls provides an interchange between the Elizabeth Line and existing Northern and Central lines. The 250-metre (825-foot) platform and station located 24 metres below ground is about the length of Wembley Football Stadium. Construction work has been undertaken in front of the Centre Point multi-storey office building in a protected conservation area with heritage listed buildings, businesses, shops, restaurants, and other amenities. Components and prefabricated structures had to be delivered to the site and excavated materials removed with as little disruption as possible to central London. Many passengers using London's Northern and Central lines through the existing Tottenham Court Road Station were unaware of what was going on behind a hoarding in front of the Crossrail building works. When complete, more than 200,000 passengers are expected to pass through the new station every day.

10. Crossrail's tunnelling machine makes breakthrough into the City of London, 40 metres below ground under Liverpool Street Station.

with the 'lonely project', such as: How do individuals, teams, and organizations involved in projects learn from the past? How do they develop their knowledge and prepare for the future?

No project is an island

Over the past two decades, researchers have provided insights, frameworks, and perspectives on how organizations work together in projects and how projects are embedded in organizations. This research first emerged in Scandinavia in the early 1990s, possibly because these countries have a disproportionately large number of project-based firms in complex engineering industries—such as Ericsson, ABB, Saab, Skanska, Statoil, and Nokia—with close ties to local universities. In what became known as the 'Scandinavian School of Project Studies', project management (Chapter 3), organizational theory (Chapter 4), innovation management (Chapter 5), and other streams of literature were used to undertake in-depth studies of how projects evolve in different contexts.

While its roots were in Scandinavia, the field of project studies expanded in the late 1990s when scholars elsewhere in the world began to discover that many firms and industries are project based. These studies shared the view that traditional writings on project management were too narrowly concerned with producing handbooks on how to manage a project, programme, or portfolio, rather than how projects shape—and are shaped by—the wider development of organizations, industries, and society. Matts Engwall expressed it well when he said that 'no project is an island': what goes on inside a project must be understood in relation to previous, current, and future projects, and the wider institutional context within which it is undertaken.

A project is a temporary organization and designed to dissolve when its task is accomplished, whereas a firm is a permanent organization which is established to grow, prosper, and survive indefinitely. Jörg Sydow and his co-authors suggest that this temporary and permanent context creates the two fundamental tensions or dilemmas associated with project-based organizing.

The 'autonomy versus integration' dilemma is between the autonomous requirements of each project and the need to integrate projects in the wider organization. The focused, fast, and autonomous work undertaken in a particular project serves to create new knowledge and innovation for each client (Chapter 5), but may not align with the strategic priorities of the parent organization within which the project is embedded. BAA recognized this tension when the T5 project was established as a standalone organization with autonomy and resources required to manage such a complex programme of work, but with a direct line of reporting to the executive team to ensure that the project was tightly integrated into Heathrow's corporate activities.

The 'doing versus learning' dilemma is between creating new knowledge to address the immediate demands of a project and using the learning gained to improve the performance of projects undertaken in future by the parent organization. In the traditional project management literature, projects are generally treated as unique, non-recurring, and undertaken in isolation from previous or future projects. This 'every project is unique' mindset encourages organizations to believe that there is little point in capturing the learning gained in one project and repeating successful practices on subsequent projects. Consequently, firms often suffer from organizational amnesia when it comes to transferring knowledge from one project to the next and to the wider organization (Box 10).

The two dilemmas are interwoven in practice because, as Sydow and his co-authors point out, being focused means that team members may be less interested in things taking place outside the project; being fast means that people have little time to reflect on their work and record lessons learnt; and being autonomous means that the project team may develop into a silo of learning,

Box 10 Unique and repetitive projects

Projects involve a spectrum of tasks ranging from unique to repetitive. A unique task is for a one-time situation and requires visionary, flexible, creative actions, and real-time learning. A repetitive task has been performed many times in the past (standardized procedures such as bidding, cost control, and risk management) with established clients and will be undertaken repeatedly in the future. People know what to do, how to do it, and share similar experiences and interpretations of the situation. We can only really understand whether a project as a whole is unique or repetitive by placing it in the wider historical context. Some projects really are unique undertakings if they represent an entirely new experience for the parent organization, whereas many others are repetitive because they show little deviation from projects performed in the past.

forcing others to 'reinvent the wheel' and restricting the flow of knowledge to other projects and the firm as a whole.

It is now recognized that no single species of organization—such as the adhocracy—captures the variety of organizations involved in projects. In their book *Managing and Working in Project Society* (2015), Rolf Lundin and his co-authors identify several different forms of project organization and discuss how they differ from those that prevailed during the industrial age. Here we refer to a simple matrix originally developed by Jonas Söderlund to highlight some of the distinctive temporary and permanent forms of project-based organizing (Figure 11). By distinguishing between single and multiple projects and between single and multiple organizations (e.g. firms and government agencies), the matrix helps us identify four broad categories of project organizing: single-project organizations, project-based organizations, project networks, and project ecologies. All four exist in some form or another in most industries and encompass a variety of firms, government agencies, joint ventures, public–private partnerships, and other structures.

	One organization	**Many organizations**
One project	Single-project organization	Project network
Many projects	Project-based organization	Project ecology

11. **Forms of project organizing.**

Single-project organizations

A single-project organization is established as a one-time legal or financial entity to achieve a specific goal and designed to dissolve when the task has been accomplished. It inherits its strategic purpose and funding and is not usually required to generate further revenues until the task is completed—although additional injections of money may be needed when the project is under way. When an aircraft carrier, movie, hospital, or high-speed railway link is completed, the single-project organization ceases to exist. Some can last for as little as a few weeks or months (e.g. a feature film), but organizations with a duration of ten years or more are not uncommon in large public infrastructure and military projects.

The single-project organization has little time to develop the 'organizational memory', routines, and capabilities that firms like Microsoft, Sony, and Google rely upon to survive, grow, and prosper in a changing competitive environment. Any knowledge and learning acquired and developed during the project generally disappears when the organization is disbanded on completion of its task. There is also much less time to cultivate personal relationships and build trust that people develop in firms over years and decades. Yet studies of independent film producers—an extreme example of a single-project organization—have shown that people can develop 'swift trust' to compensate for working for the organizational equivalent of a 'one-night stand'. Unlike the major studios (e.g. Disney), an independent film company is established to make a single movie and disbands when the film is released. Members of a film crew assembled to produce the movie are able to trust each other and coordinate complex interdependent tasks because they have clearly defined expertise and professional roles (e.g. production, photography, and set design). Each member of the project knows their role, has performed a specialized task repeatedly in the past, and is able to do so again when working with new and familiar crew members.

Various forms of single-project organizations have been created to manage large public infrastructure projects in London including public–private partnerships (PPP), special-purpose vehicles (SPV), client bodies, and delivery partners. As we saw in Chapter 1, a number of consortiums have been awarded PPP contracts to design, build, finance, operate, and maintain London's tube lines, railways, and hospitals. Rail Link Engineering (an incorporated contract between Arup, Bechtel, Halcrow, and Systra) was formed as an SPV in 1996 to manage the design and construction of High-Speed 1 (HS1)—the 109-kilometre (65-mile) high-speed railway between the Channel Tunnel and London St Pancras station. Established as a fully autonomous legal entity, the risks associated with an SPV can be isolated and considered to pose less of a threat to the sponsor or parent organization than would the establishment of a new business unit or division.

The Olympic Delivery Authority (ODA) was created in 2006 by Act of Parliament as a temporary public body accountable to its sponsors—the government and the Greater London Authority. The Act provided the ODA with the legal power and responsibilities to construct the infrastructure and venues for the Games. The ODA, which employed around 220 staff, recognized that a delivery organization could not be established in-house with available resources or in the time available, so decided to appoint a 'delivery partner' to manage the programme: a private sector consortium called 'CLM' employing over 500 staff at its peak seconded from the three parent firms of CH2M, Laing O'Rourke, and Mace. CLM was selected because the parent firms in this joint venture had proven capabilities in managing previous Olympic construction programmes and large infrastructure projects (including Heathrow Terminal 5). The ODA and CLM reduced significantly in size after the Games started on 27 July 2012 and were eventually dissolved: CLM in March 2013 and the ODA in December 2014.

The Crossrail project could have been undertaken as part of the Transport for London (TfL) programme of activities, but there was a concern that the progress of such a high-profile endeavour might be jeopardized if the wider needs of TfL were to take priority over those of the project. Crossrail Limited was, therefore, established as a separate company to ensure that the people responsible for its delivery were entirely focused on a single task, with a clear remit and clarity of purpose. An integrated programme delivery team of around 1,200 staff was formed including the client (Crossrail Limited) and two delivery partners: a programme partner called Transcend (a joint venture between CH2M, AECOM, and The Nichols Group) and a project delivery partner called Crossrail Central (a joint venture led by Bechtel and supported by Halcrow and Systra) to manage the construction of the complex central section of tunnels. As the project moved towards completion, the operator (Rail for London) became a more active member of the integrated programme delivery team. When the project is completed in 2019, the client and delivery partner organizations will be disbanded.

Project-based organizations

Many firms depend on projects to create and develop new products and services in competitive and fast-changing markets, but their core business is high-volume operations (Chapter 1). A firm or an organization is 'project-based' when most of its design, development, and productive activities are handled as projects for clients and are embedded in a permanent organization which is expected to remain in business and find new work when each project is completed. In most cases, employees in project-based organizations have relatively stable positions and many have long-term exclusive contracts.

Building on Mintzberg's observation (Chapter 4), we distinguish between two types of project-based organization. Those organized to address their own in-house needs for projects include a number of large private companies (e.g. Shell and BP in the oil and gas industry), government agencies, and publicly funded organizations as diverse as the US Department of Defense, NASA, and TfL. Those serving external clients, by contrast, are widespread in industries that produce customized products and services as one-off units or in small batches. They include capital goods (e.g. defence, aerospace, factory automation systems, rolling stock, nuclear power stations, oil and gas platforms, shipbuilding, software, and telecommunications), creative industries (e.g. film studios, music, video games, and TV production), public infrastructure (e.g. hospitals, roads, railways, and schools), professional services (e.g. advertising and consulting), construction and architecture, and high-value bespoke products (e.g. Formula One racing cars, private jets, and luxury yachts).

Project-based organizations are sometimes nested within the divisions, business units, and subsidiaries of large firms and departments of government. The continuing survival and growth of a diversified firm like Toshiba, the Tokyo-headquartered global corporation, depends on substantial high-volume production operations (e.g. consumer electronics and household appliances) and securing a series of major projects in high-value capital goods (e.g. high-speed rail transportation and nuclear power plants). Government agencies responsible for railways, roads, water, and other utility networks have large organizations to operate and provide services and internal project-based divisions to procure and manage major projects in collaboration with private sector contractors. The London Underground (a subsidiary of TfL), for example, is responsible for operating tube trains and stations and managing major capital projects, such as the construction of new lines or refurbishment of stations.

Frequently found in construction, architecture, and professional services, the activities of a project-based firm are based entirely on managing dozens, hundreds, if not thousands of projects at any particular time. They have to balance the discontinuous requirements of each project and the firm's longer-term strategic business objectives. Bechtel, the large American civil engineering, construction, and project management firm, for example, has been prime contractor on some of the world's largest projects such as the Hoover Dam, San Francisco's Bay Area Rapid Transit system, Boston Central Artery/Tunnel, Channel Tunnel, Jubilee Line Extension, and Crossrail. Employing about 55,000 people to manage about 25,000 projects in 160 countries in 2016, Bechtel has the breadth of capabilities to handle multiple aspects of large-scale projects, including project planning, financing, procurement, design, construction, and management of contractors.

Various structures are used to coordinate projects embedded in project-based firms, ranging from functional (where projects are undertaken by one or more groups or departments) at one extreme to dedicated project-based organizations at the other (Chapter 3). Many, like Arup, have some form of matrix structure to combine functional and project activities. Whereas pure project-based organizations are good at problem-solving, advancing innovation, and focusing on the individual requirements of each client, they are less effective than matrix structures when it comes to coordinating resources, sharing knowledge across projects embedded in the parent organization, and achieving organization-wide efficiency gains. Many organizational units in project-based firms are led by powerful individuals—whom David Gann and his co-authors call 'project barons'—who compete for resources to support their existing and new entrepreneurial initiatives.

When projects are similar and repetitive, a project-based organization can develop the intellectual resources, expertise, and routines required to win, coordinate, and efficiently execute multiple projects in a technology or market base. When project tasks are repeated, organizations with 'project capabilities' can perform tasks more reliably and efficiently. Project capabilities are comprised of tacit knowledge (or personal experience) possessed by members of project teams and the codified (or explicit) knowledge embodied in standardized project management procedures, processes, tools, and guidebooks. When Sir John Egan joined BAA from his previous position as CEO of Jaguar Motors, for example, he found to his surprise that every project in airport construction was 'treated as a blank sheet of paper' and newly assembled teams 'tended to think it through from first principles over and over again'. To discourage managers from treating each project as unique, BAA developed capabilities embodied in a guidebook (based on lean processes used by Japanese car producers) to perform standardized and repeatable time-sequenced tasks, milestones, and stage-gates and deliver cost-effective, profitable projects.

A firm's project capabilities are occasionally reconfigured to keep pace with a changing environment when a 'vanguard project' is created to achieve a breakthrough innovation, as illustrated by Arup's Dongtan project and attempts to grow a sustainable urban design business (Chapter 4). A sign of how technologies and markets will evolve in the future, vanguard projects often reveal the fragility of an organization's existing project capabilities, developed over many years to execute projects for a stable group of clients and markets. Members of a vanguard project explore alternative approaches, engage in trial-and-error learning, and often ignore established procedures to create new offerings, anticipate progress, capture innovative thinking, and develop new project management structures, tools, and processes. Vanguard projects sometimes mark the beginning of a 'project epoch' when a new-type project emerges and takes hold, lasting years or decades, to address the fairly predictable and well-understood requirements of established clients.

In a process of project-capability building, the new knowledge created in a vanguard project may be developed and reused across projects to support a firm's growth in a new market. For example, Heathrow T5 was a vanguard project for Laing O'Rourke, the largest firm by contract value involved in the construction of the new terminal. Working closely with BAA and other suppliers, Laing O'Rourke helped identify, develop, and introduce many innovative processes used to deliver the T5 project such as integrated project team working, digital design technology, project collaboration software, and offsite prefabrication. The capabilities that Laing O'Rourke gained on T5 were developed, honed, and improved further when the firm went on to become the leading contractor and delivery partner on a series of megaprojects in London (e.g. St Pancras railway redevelopment, London 2012 Olympics, and Crossrail) and elsewhere in the world.

Project networks

Many projects involve some form of collaboration with external parties and the most complex projects have to coordinate large networks—or temporary coalitions—of contractors and subcontractors. The word 'network' conveys the idea that a project consists of many organizations working on a joint task for a defined period of time. It draws attention to the relationships or ties and the frequency, duration, and density of interactions among individual and organizational members of a project.

Project networks are found in a great variety of private and public sectors such as aerospace, oil and gas platforms, defence, university research, advertising, biotechnology, and construction. They range in size from small projects with a few partners to megaprojects like the T5, HS1, London 2012 Olympics, and Crossrail involving dozens of contractors and thousands of subcontractors. They also vary in duration from as little as the days, weeks, or months needed to make a TV documentary to several decades in some major defence systems projects such as the development of the Joint Strike Fighter programme, which began in 1993 and has still not entered service. Organizations often play different roles during the life of a project network. In large civil engineering projects, for example, the client organization, prime contractor, or delivery partner remains in place for the full duration, while other organizations are brought in for specific phases, such as design or construction.

In large project networks, one or more organizations leads the endeavour and coordinates and schedules the activities undertaken by multiple parties. As we have seen in Chapter 3, capabilities in systems integration (a practice pioneered by US defence and aerospace firms) are particularly important in complex projects. A client organization can develop these capabilities in-house, appoint a prime contractor, or work with a delivery partner. The London 2012 Olympics, for example, consisted of more than 70 individual projects managed by principal contractors including design and construction of 14 temporary (e.g. International Broadcast Centre) and permanent buildings (e.g. Olympics Stadium, Velodrome, and Aquatics Centre), 20 km of roads, 26 bridges, 13 km of tunnels, and 80 hectares of parkland and utilities infrastructure. Working closely together, the client (the ODA) and its delivery partner (CLM) coordinated the design, construction, integration, and delivery of the venues and infrastructure. The ODA was responsible for the overall progress of the project and dealing with external stakeholders and neighbours impacted by it. CLM managed the programme and principal contractors responsible for each major venue, coordinated the interfaces between them, integrated them into the Olympic Park infrastructure, and prepared for the staging of the Games.

In addition to these coordination challenges, mechanisms are needed to build cooperation among the participants in a project network. In recent years, sponsors of the UK's large infrastructure projects have attempted to establish more collaborative relationships between clients and contractors. Following BAA's pioneering approach on T5, more enlightened clients no longer rely exclusively on fixed-price contracts for complex projects which penalize contractors for delays, promote adversarial relationships, and often lead to irreconcilable conflict. Like Heathrow Airport, clients are adopting relational contracts that build long-term cooperation with their suppliers, with a balanced mix of incentives and penalties to reduce opportunism and reward innovation and problem-solving. Similar forms of cooperation exist elsewhere in the world such as the 'Integrated Program Team' in the United States and 'Alliancing' in Australia.

On Crossrail, for example, a judicious balance has to be found between the differing objectives, time horizons, and priorities of the client and its contractors. The client delivery organization is focused on the long-term goals of finishing the project on time, safely, and within budget, dealing with external stakeholders, and handing over a 'world-class railway' to the operator, whereas the more immediate priority of each contractor is to complete a discrete piece of work and make a profit. Crossrail has over sixty major contracts with individual firms and joint ventures to construct the railway, such as the £400 million western tunnel contract awarded to the BAM Nuttall, Ferrovial, and Kier (BFK) joint venture. Contracts range in size from as little as £1 million for design services to over £500 million for the largest tunnelling and systems contracts. The client relies on collaborative contracts and various forms of persuasion and personal relationships to motivate the contractors (if necessary talking directly with the contractor's CEO to wield influence) and keep the project on track towards completion. To overcome problems and resolve disputes, members of Crossrail's delivery partner also work onsite with contractors in co-located integrated project teams.

Achieving cooperation is particularly challenging in 'global projects' ranging from activities undertaken in a specific geographical location (e.g. the London 2012 Olympics) to spatially dispersed project teams at multiple locations around the world (e.g. the Boeing 777 project). As firms outsource and internationalize their activities, global projects have become what Richard Scott and his co-authors describe as the 'nexus of inter-organizational cooperation in a global marketplace'. Aligning the interests of participants is difficult in global projects because they are so institutionally complex, culturally diverse, and often conflict-ridden. Participants from various organizational and cultural backgrounds inhabit different 'thought worlds' that often create frictions when teams are co-located. CH2M, for example, found that working in a co-located integrated project team—as it did so successfully during the London 2012 Olympics project—was particularly challenging in the cross-cultural setting of the $5.35 billion project initiated in 2006 to expand and modernize the Panama Canal. Conflicts soon appeared after the local client (Autoridad del Canal de Panamá) hired CH2M, the American-based global engineering firm, to jointly manage the Panama Canal expansion project. Negotiations about who should lead the project and be accountable for the outcome were sometimes tense and difficult to resolve, in part because the two parties had such different expectations and institutional and cultural backgrounds.

Project ecologies

The organizations we have been discussing are often participants in industries—as diverse as aerospace, advertising, software, and consulting—that depend on projects to undertake most of their productive activities. Various terms—such as project business network, geographical cluster, and ecosystem—are used to describe the constellation of organizations involved in each other's past, current, and future projects. They may include clients, contractors, subcontractors, consultants, manufacturers, financiers, universities, funding bodies, and other stakeholders. In project-based industries, organizations enter into various forms of collaborative partnerships or arm's-length contractual relationships with participants in some projects, whilst competing to win new contracts and improve their competitive advantage in others. Relationships between entities often alter from one project to the next. For example, suppliers of railway rolling stock, such as Alstom, Bombardier, Toshiba, or Siemens, may be a prime contractor on one urban railway system project and subcontractor on another. Government agencies often play a pivotal role as project sponsor and client in public sector projects (e.g. highways, railways, and healthcare) to ensure that public and private parties work together to achieve public policy objectives.

Learning and capability development is possible in project-based industries because the enduring relationships and trust established among the participants collaborating in projects provide a repository of shared learning and prior experience which can be retrieved when participants work together in the future. The experience gained while working together—known as the 'shadow of the past'—often decides which participants will be selected to work on future projects. The expectations and hope that participants will work together again—known as the 'shadow of the future'—is an incentive to behave and perform well on a current project. BAA, for example, established five-year 'framework agreements' to build constructive relationships with suppliers involved in current and future projects at Heathrow and other airports. Treating its suppliers as long-term partners in a stream of projects reduced BAA's coordination costs and provided suppliers with the stability they needed to develop the capabilities and improve their performance over time.

Gernot Grabher introduced the concept of a 'project ecology' to describe the dense network of personal ties, organizational, and institutional relationships found in geographical clusters of project-based activities, such as the advertising agencies concentrated in the Soho district of London or the vast mobilization of people, firms, and bodies required to plan and build the London 2012 Olympic Games. The four layers of a project ecology—the core team, the firm, epistemic community, and personal networks—provide a deep pool of personal, organizational, and institutional capabilities and memory of project experiences that can be retrieved and mobilized to manage current projects and prepare for the future (Box 11).

Some of the grandest civil engineering projects in living memory have been undertaken in London since the start of the 21st century to renew and expand the city's ageing Victorian

Box 11 Layers of a project ecology

The core team layer refers to the professional roles and tasks performed by individuals and how they collaborate in project teams. In a 'cumulative ecology', teams remain stable over successive projects to achieve incremental improvements in performance. In a 'disruptive ecology', the composition of the team is altered to combine people with fresh ideas needed to create radical change.

The firm layer refers to the project capabilities (see 'Project-based organizations') which are required to improve performance by repeating practices that worked well in the past. New combinations of technologies and practices are pulled together when innovative solutions are needed to address challenging client demands, such as BAA's T5 project.

The epistemic community layer refers to the knowledge, extending beyond the boundary of the firm, that professionals in client, supplier, or corporate groups establish to share non-confidential information, case studies, and other experiences.

The personal network layer refers to the relationships and ties among individuals that extend beyond projects and business relationships. Often remaining in the project background, this layer is activated when people are called upon to solve specific problems or to provide support and advice when needed.

infrastructure, develop entire urban districts, and build new air and railway transportation links. They include high-profile projects such as HS1, T5, London 2012 Olympics, Crossrail, Thames Tideway Tunnel, High-Speed 2 (the multi-billion-pound high-speed railway from London Euston via Birmingham to Leeds and Manchester). The expanding network of individuals, teams, contractors, and clients working on these projects and circulating between them has helped to establish London's thriving megaproject ecology and worldwide reputation for innovative project delivery models.

With head offices in and around London, architecture, consultancy, construction, programme management, and civil engineering firms—such as Rogers Stirk Harbour + Partners, Arup, Balfour Beatty, Mace, Costain, CH2M, and Laing O'Rourke—are located in close proximity to each other. Because of their heavy dependence on government infrastructure contracts, senior executives in these firms have cultivated close relationships with project sponsors, government officials, and political leaders. They are the first to hear about new proposals and are in a strong position to bid for new work, often in collaboration with one of their local partners. Firms that have successfully developed their capabilities and reputation on one megaproject tend to reappear in different guises in the future. Laing O'Rourke, for example, was the largest contractor on T5, London 2012's delivery partner, the contractor appointed to build Crossrail's Tottenham Court Road Station, and part of the consortium building the central section of the Thames Tideway Tunnel. Core teams in firms and client bodies often migrate from one project to the next. For example, after completing its work for London 2012, the ODA's entire procurement team went on to work for Crossrail.

Many individuals—at all levels from senior executives to project managers and operatives—are 'project nomads', developing knowledge and sharing expertise as they move between London's megaprojects. For example, Andrew Wolstenholme, the project director of T5, went on to become CEO of Crossrail, Andy Mitchell, the programme director of Crossrail, became CEO of the Thames Tideway Tunnel, and Mark Thurston, a senior programme manager on London 2012 and Crossrail, became CEO of High-Speed 2. Often their professional identities are more closely tied to the project than to the permanent organization that employs them. Managers working for CLM, London 2012's delivery partner, had to get used to 'wearing two hats': they knew that they would eventually rejoin their parent firms, but identified closely with the project while it was under way. Personal ties and relations between individuals who have worked together in the past permeate each new megaproject, encouraging the circulation of knowledge, ideas, and successful practices.

Several of London's megaprojects have recently promoted the idea of creating a systematic and formal approach to harness innovation to complete projects more efficiently and create better outcomes—something achieved informally on the Erie Canal project (Chapter 2). In 2013, Crossrail established an innovation programme encouraging contractors, suppliers, and other stakeholders in the project to develop, implement, and share new ideas, technologies, and practices An in-house team managed the innovation programme and established a database to capture all the innovative ideas, proposals, and solutions submitted by members of the project. In October 2016, the CEOs of Crossrail and the Thames Tideway Tunnel projects used their personal networks and relationships to form a client-led epistemic community called the 'Infrastructure Industry Innovation Platform' supported by major contractors, a government funding body, and leading universities. To prevent innovation from occurring in isolation on each megaproject—as it had in the past—the platform (which builds on a database and collaborative approach originally created for Crossrail) was established to share new ideas, practices, and technologies with other megaprojects in London and elsewhere in the UK.

In Chapter 7 we consider whether these new and emerging forms of project organization will be able to deal with the major challenges societies are facing in the 21st century.

Chapter 7
Back to the future

Project management came of age during and after the Second World War when the systems approach was invented to coordinate and schedule the development of weapons and aerospace systems. The traditional, systems-based model, formalized in the late 1960s and 1970s by professional bodies to bring coherence, standardized procedures and discipline to the management of projects, was based on the expectation that markets and technologies were well understood and projects could be carefully prepared to accommodate stable and predictable conditions. The assumption behind this model, that all projects can be managed in a similar way, has been questioned in recent books and articles that urge us to rethink, reinvent, and reconstruct project management. Few of today's projects are predictable and unchanging. In most cases, plans have to be realistic and flexible to address a future that cannot be fully known at the outset and adjustable and responsive to unexpected, novel, and fast-changing conditions arising when a project is under way. It is now recognized that an adaptive model of project management supported by digital technologies is required for the complex, innovative, and unpredictable projects of the 21st century. Yet the idea that projects are shaped by the dynamics of the environment within which they are planned and executed is not a new one. The leaders of America's early weapons systems projects—Groves, Schriever, Ramo, Raborn, and Webb—understood that the extent of uncertainty, complexity, and urgency varies for different kinds of projects and each project has to be managed in a flexible and adaptive way. Until recently it seems project management had forgotten its roots.

Wicked problems

The trend towards project-based organizing is increasing in the 21st century as managers recognize that innovation is the norm in competitive global markets and organizations expect to have to manage a continuing stream of projects. Large-scale organizations are increasingly infiltrated by transient project organizations, groups, and teams that spring up in their midst and then disappear. Organizations that are good at learning from the past, building project capabilities, and working with partners in adaptive, collaborative teams will be better prepared for the future. But will existing project management structures, processes, and tools be able to cope with the difficult challenges now facing societies, such as an ageing population, poverty, terrorism, the migration and refugee crisis, and other issues?

Perhaps the most significant and challenging 'wicked problems'—difficult to define with no clear solutions—of our age result from the combination of rapid urbanization and climate change. The rise of mass production, the car and aeroplane, and a pattern of urbanization based on cheap energy powered by fossil fuels (about 80 per cent of global energy demand in 2014) set us on a path of industrialization over the past 200 years that has fundamentally changed our climate system. Current predictions suggest that at the end of the 21st century, the warming effect of greenhouse gases such as carbon dioxide and methane will create a climate that will be very different from pre-industrial conditions. Uncertainties about our future climate—arising from the complexity of the climate system and the social, political, and economic responses to it—mean that project organizations of the future might have to be even more innovative, flexible, and fast-paced.

The number of people living in cities is expected to rise to 70 per cent of the global population in 2050, from 50 per cent in 2015. A study by McKinsey Global Institute in 2013 estimates that $57 trillion will be spent on investment in the world's infrastructure between 2013 and 2030. Many infrastructure megaprojects are being initiated and executed to keep pace with the unprecedented acceleration of urbanization in newly industrializing countries like China and India. In cities like London, Berlin, and New York, they are needed to replace the ageing buildings, urban developments, and fragmented infrastructures of a past industrial age. They are needed to design and build the ecologically sustainable 'smart city' of the future using digital sensors and monitoring instruments to control transportation, communications, water, and other utilities, and make energy supply more adaptive to changing demand.

Megaprojects in densely populated urban areas might be more challenging than the systems projects of the Cold War. Although the Apollo programme was complex and uncertain, for example, it was a closed system with almost unlimited resources to achieve a clear and unwavering goal (to land a man safely on the Moon by the end of the decade), largely protected from political interference and other social, economic, and environmental pressures. Megaprojects in cities—like the Boston Big Dig and the London 2012 Olympics—are open systems. They have porous boundaries that extend beyond the system and have to accommodate multiple stakeholders with diverging, often ambiguous and conflicting interests.

Our new and reconstructed cities and infrastructures will have to be designed to be resilient to climate change and responsive when the unexpected happens, such as Japan's Fukushima nuclear accident in 2011. It is highly unlikely that a monolithic Manhattan-style project designed to achieve a single goal will be able to cope with the pervasive, diffuse, and continuously evolving problems associated with mitigating and adapting to climate change. Thomas Hughes suggested that multiple, diverse, and geographically dispersed 'eco-technological projects'—carbon capture and storage, low-cost solar battery, flood risk, tidal energy, and eco-city projects, for example—will be required to achieve the transition towards a post-industrial and ecologically sustainable society powered by low-carbon and renewable energy sources.

We end this book by considering how projects of the future might be equipped to respond to these societal challenges and the relentless pressure to innovate and compete in global markets. Many years ago, Alvin Toffler predicted that adaptive project organizations, with authority and responsibility distributed horizontally among self-motivated and knowledgeable members of problem-solving teams, would challenge and ultimately replace top–down, regimented bureaucracy as societies make the transition to a post-industrial age. Government agencies, firms, and individuals have found it difficult to adjust to this new style of organization and the transition has taken longer and may not be quite as far reaching as Toffler expected. Some of the examples and case studies described in this book provide an indication of what tomorrow's projects might look like.

Post-industrial projects

In this post-industrial future, project success will no longer be measured solely by how well the team or organization meet time, budget, and specified requirements. It will depend on whether the operational outcome creates exceptional value for sponsors, customers, operators, and users. The Gehry-designed Guggenheim Museum project in Bilbao did much more than construct an iconic building on time and within budget. It revitalized a declining industrial city. Apple's success in creating the iPod and iTunes platform changed how people listen to music and created one of the world's most successful firms. Many firms and government agencies are finding that bids specifying the required operational performance of an IT system, hospital, or railway create better and more innovative outcomes. For example, invitations to tender for a specified number of trains will produce a range of prices, but may not stimulate innovation. In contrast, demands for 'train availability'—as we saw in the case of Alstom—may result in a variety of proposals outlining novel ways to build, operate, finance, and maintain a fleet of trains over many years.

Highly capable sponsors and client organizations will spend time at the start defining the project goal and selecting the best way of achieving it. Learning systematically from previous projects helps to calibrate the risks involved, reach informed judgements about how to address them, and produce more realistic schedule and cost estimates. Faced with the uncertainties involved in building the fifth terminal at London's Heathrow Airport, BAA learned lessons from previous construction and airport projects and decided to create a flexible delivery model. It was based on an overarching flexible contract and depended on collaborative teams being able to solve emergent problems and embrace new opportunities that could not be anticipated at the outset. The London 2012 delivery model, by contrast, used a variety of contracts to target the pieces of uncertainty involved in constructing the mix of standardized and bespoke buildings and structures in the Olympic Park.

During this front-end definition period, the sponsor or parent organization will develop a compelling vision showing how the project meets the needs of existing customers or creates a new market opportunity. Operators and users will be more fully engaged at an early stage to ensure that their requirements, concerns, and priorities are fully addressed in the design of the eventual outcome. Boeing, for example, listened closely to the needs and priorities of eight major airlines to define their requirements and shape the design of the 777 aircraft. But as Elon Musk knows so well, there are times when not listening to existing customers is important. Until recently, for example, car manufacturers were reluctant to develop electric and autonomous vehicle technologies that they believed customers had no desire to purchase. The breakthrough came when the all-electric Tesla car was developed by the industry's first start company since the 1920s. As we have seen, firms competing in fast-changing markets—Apple, Microsoft, and Google—have a balanced portfolio of projects to know how to sustain existing markets and when to open up new ones.

Organizations will have dynamic and flexible teams with the capability to solve problems, innovate, and adapt as circumstances change during the planning and execution phases of a project. Project leaders will be adept at building collaborative teams and overcoming the conflicts and creative tensions that often arise when diverse groups of people with different ideas, cultural values, personalities, and competing priorities start working together. Members of Arup's Dongtan and Beijing Water Cube projects had to learn how to work together in multidisciplinary and multicultural teams—in co-located offices and distributed across continents—that emerged and dissolved in response to the changing needs of demanding clients and unexpected problems that were identified as the work progressed. Lean and agile processes may spread to industries where project teams competing in fast-changing, innovative markets have to develop alternative solutions in parallel, work concurrently, and adapt in real time to the feedback from frequent interactions with customers and executive sponsors.

In the past, megaprojects sometimes incorporated new technology in the design of an infrastructure system (e.g. advanced signalling technology on London's Jubilee Line), but rarely experimented with new ideas, practices, and technologies once the project was under way. Innovation during execution was considered an unnecessary downside risk associated with delays and cost overruns. Tomorrow's sponsors and clients, by contrast, will embrace innovation as an upside opportunity to design better outcomes and complete megaprojects more efficiently. They will know that performance can be improved by using existing knowledge and adopting proven technologies that worked well elsewhere. But they will recognize that the uncertainties involved in experimenting with new technologies and practices can be minimized prior to their introduction by undertaking trials to develop, test, rehearse, and learn about alternative solutions. The innovation programme established by Crossrail to create, share, and implement new and existing technologies, ideas, and practices, for example, is now being applied on other megaprojects in London and elsewhere.

The systems integrator of the future will have to design and integrate increasingly complex and interdependent infrastructure systems. Many complex projects—the construction of high-rise buildings and nuclear power plants, for instance—will be modular, using flexible combinations of standardized components produced more cheaply and with greater precision in offsite factories and assembled more safely and efficiently when brought together onsite. Each part of a project—components, subsystems, and systems—will be designed to work as an integrated whole and achieve targets for sustainable low-carbon and efficient operational performance. Arup does this when it delineates how the social and technical components and systems of an ecologically sustainable or smart city—such as water, energy, transport, governance, culture, education, telecommunications, and housing—will interact when the entire system of systems becomes operational. The integrator will be more fully engaged with stakeholders inside and outside the systems they are building. On several of London's megaprojects, a client organization provides a single point of contact for all external relationships with government agencies, local authorities, utilities, businesses, communities, and other stakeholders, while a delivery partner focuses inwardly on managing the programme of interdependent activities undertaken by a large network of contractors and subcontractors.

Supported by digital technology, tomorrow's projects will be alive with the information and data required to coordinate the design, construction, handover, and operation of products and systems and respond in real time to any changes in circumstances. Co-located and geographically dispersed virtual teams sharing the same digital model can visualize the final design of complex products, detect interference and clashes between components prior to their integration, test virtual prototypes, and identify the latest moment a design can be changed before moving to fabrication and construction. The usefulness of digital technology extends to the operation and maintenance of an asset by creating a database showing the exact location of components such as the cabling, heating, and cooling systems of a building. Frank Gehry is using his own Digital Project software to control construction costs in a collaborative process where the traditional boundaries between designer, constructor, and user continue to blur. In future, projects might use 'augmented reality' headset technology that is able to supplement the real world by laying computer-generated images on top of it. Equipped with smart glasses, designers can inspect a product from different vantage points, lay three-dimensional images onto it, and rearrange the position of virtual components. AECOM, the global firm of architects and engineers, for example, uses the HoloLens headset produced by Microsoft to help designers walk around and review the digital representation of a building with complex geometry.

For the individual working in projects, the post-industrial future brings new threats and opportunities. Many organizations will be filled with transient teams and extremely mobile individuals. Relationships with colleagues will be less permanent, more temporary than in the past. People will develop quick and intense relationships on each temporary endeavour, and learn to bear the loss of more enduring ones. They must get used to being frequently reassigned and shuffled about from one project to another. With each new change, individuals must reorient themselves. Each change brings the need for new learning and may strain the adaptability of the individual, creating social and psychological tensions. But others may thrive in this temporary and fast-changing world. Whereas careers were once defined by loyalty to one or more permanent organizations, a growing number of people will happily move from one project to the next throughout their working lives. As Toffler predicted, projects will be attractive to individuals who want to work in challenging and creative environments where they can 'play with problems' and are encouraged to innovate. They will begin to think about their work, daily activities, and even their personal ambitions as projects.

Further reading

Chapter 1: Introduction

A. Davies, T. Brady, and M. Hobday, 'Charting a path toward integrated solutions', *MIT Sloan Management Review*, Spring (2006), 39–48.

D. Defoe, *An Essay Upon Projects* (Rockville, Md.: Arc Manor, 1697; repr. 2008).

The Economist, 'Project management: overdue and over budget, over and over again', 11 June (2005), 65–6.

B. Flyvbjerg, 'What you should know about megaprojects and why: an overview', *Project Management Journal*, 45(2) (2014), 6–19.

P. Hall, *Great Planning Disasters* (Harmondsworth: Penguin Books, 1980).

T. Heatherwick, *Thomas Heatherwick: Making* (London: Thames & Hudson, 2012).

T. P. Hughes, *Rescuing Prometheus* (New York: Pantheon Books, 1998).

R. A. Lundin, N. Arvidsson, T. Brady, E. Ekstedt, C. Midler, and J. Sydow, *Managing and Working in Project Society: Institutional Challenges of Temporary Organizations* (Cambridge: Cambridge University Press, 2015).

P. W. G. Morris and G. H. Hough, *The Anatomy of Major Projects* (Chichester: John Wiley & Sons, 1987).

T. Peters and R. H. Waterman, *In Search of Excellence: Lessons from America's Best-Run Companies* (New York: Harper & Row, 1982).

W. A. Randolph and B. Z. Posner, 'What every manager needs to know about project management', *Sloan Management Review*, 65 (1988), 65–73.

P. Scranton, 'Projects as a focus for historical analysis: surveying the landscape', *History and Technology*, 30(4) (2014), 354–73.

A. J. Shenhar and D. Dvir, *Reinventing Project Management: The Diamond Approach to Successful Growth and Innovation* (Boston: Harvard Business School Press, 2007).

A. Toffler, *Future Shock* (New York: Bantam Books, 1970).

A. Toffler, *The Third Wave* (New York: Bantam Books, 1980).

A. Toffler, *The Adaptive Corporation* (London: Pan Books, 1985).

Chapter 2: America's venture into the unknown

P. L. Bernstein, *Wedding the Waters: The Erie Canal and the Making of a Great Nation* (New York: W. W. Norton & Company, 2005).

B. Flyvbjerg, 'What you should know about megaprojects and why: an overview', *Project Management Journal*, 45(2) (2014), 6–19.

B. Flyvbjerg, N. Bruzelius, and W. Rothengatter, *Megaprojects and Risk: An Anatomy of Ambition* (Cambridge: Cambridge University Press, 2003).

A. O. Hirschman, *Development Projects Observed* (Washington, DC: The Brookings Institution, 1967).

G. Koeppel, *Bond of Union: Building the Erie Canal and the American Empire* (Cambridge, Mass.: Da Capo Press, 2009).

R. Miller and D. R. Lessard, *The Strategic Management of Large Engineering Projects: Shaping Institutions, Risks, and Governance* (Cambridge, Mass.: The MIT Press, 2000).

P. W. G. Morris, *The Management of Projects* (London: Thomas Telford, 1994).

J. Ross and B. M. Staw, 'Organizational escalation and exit: lessons from the Shoreham Nuclear Power Plant', *Academy of Management Journal*, 36(4) (1993), 701–32.

Z. Shapira and D. J. Berndt, 'Managing grand-scale construction projects: a risk-taking perspective', *Research in Organizational Behavior*, 19 (1997), 303–60.

R. E. West, *Erie Water West: A History of the Erie Canal, 1792–1854* (Lexington, Ky: University Press of Kentucky, 1966).

Chapter 3: From Manhattan to the Moon

T. P. Hughes, *American Genesis: A History of the American Genius for Invention* (Harmondsworth: Penguin Books, 1989).

T. P. Hughes, *Rescuing Prometheus* (New York: Pantheon Books, 1998).

S. B. Johnson, 'Three approaches to big technology: operations research, systems engineering, and project management', *Technology and Culture*, 38(4) (1997), 891–919.

S. B. Johnson, *The Secret of Apollo: Systems Management in American and European Space Programs* (Baltimore: Johns Hopkins University Press, 2002).

S. Lenfle and C. Loch, 'Lost roots: how project management came to emphasize control over flexibility and novelty', *California Management Review*, 53(1) (2010), 32–55.

P. W. G. Morris, *Reconstructing Project Management* (Chichester: Wiley-Blackwell, 2013).

S. Ramo, *The Business of Science: Winning and Losing in the High-Tech Age* (New York: Hill and Wang, 1988).

H. M. Sapolsky, *The Polaris System Development: Bureaucratic and Programmatic Success in Government* (Cambridge, Mass.: Harvard University Press, 1972).

L. R. Sayles and M. K. Chandler, *Managing Large Systems: Organizations for the Future* (New Brunswick, NJ: Transaction Publications, 1971).

J. E. Webb, *Space Age Management: The Large-Scale Approach* (New York: McGraw-Hill Company, 1969).

Chapter 4: Arup's adhocracy and projects in theory

T. J. Allen, *Managing the Flow of Technology* (Cambridge, Mass.: The MIT Press, 1984).

W. Bennis, *Beyond Bureaucracy: Essays on the Development and Evolution of Human Organization* (San Francisco: Jossey-Bass Publishers, 1966).

S. Brusoni and A. Prencipe, 'Unpacking the black box of modularity: technology, products and organization', *Industrial and Corporate Change*, 10(1) (2001), 179–205.

T. Burns and G. M. Stalker, *The Management of Innovation* (Oxford: Oxford University Press, 1961).

A. De Meyer, C. Loch, and M. T. Pich, 'Managing project uncertainty', *Sloan Management Review*, 43(2) (2002), 6–67.

The Economist, 'A Chinese eco-city. City of Dreams', 21 March (2009), 68–9.

A. Edmondson, *Teaming: How Organizations Learn, Innovate, and Compete in the Knowledge Economy* (San Francisco: John Wiley & Sons, 2012).

A. Edmondson, 'Teamwork on the fly', *Harvard Business Review*, April (2012), 72–80.

K. M. Eisenhardt and B. N. Tabrizi, 'Accelerating adaptive processes: product innovation in the global computer industry', *Administrative Science Quarterly*, 40 (1995), 84–110.

J. R. Galbraith, *Designing Complex Organizations* (Reading, Mass.: Addison-Wesley, 1973).

C. J. G. Gersick, 'Pacing strategic change: the case of a new venture', *Academy of Management Journal*, 37(1) (1994), 9–45.

C. Jones and B. Lichtenstein, 'Temporary inter-organizational projects: how temporal and social embeddedness enhance coordination and manage uncertainty', in S. Cropper, C. Huxman, M. Ebers, and P. Smith Ring (eds), *The Oxford Handbook of Inter-Organizational Relations* (Oxford: Oxford University Press, 2008), 231–55.

P. Jones, *Ove Arup: Masterbuilder of the Twentieth Century* (New Haven: Yale University Press, 2006).

P. R. Lawrence and J. W. Lorsch, *Organization and Environment: Managing Differentiation and Integration* (Boston: Harvard Business School Press, 1967).

L. Lindkvist, J. Söderlund, and F. Tell, 'Managing product development projects: on the significance of fountains and deadlines', *Organization Studies*, 19 (1998), 931–51.

C. Loch, A. De Meyer, and M. T. Pich, *Managing the Unknown: A New Approach to Managing High Uncertainty and Risk in Projects* (Hoboken, NJ: John Wiley and Sons, 2006).

H. Mintzberg, *The Structuring of Organizations* (New York: Prentice-Hall, 1979).

A. Prencipe, A. Davies, and M. Hobday, *The Business of Systems Integration* (Oxford: Oxford University Press, 2003).

J. Sapsed and A. Salter, 'Postcards from the edge: local communities, global programs and boundary objects', *Organization Studies*, 25(9) (2005), 1515–34.

L. R. Sayles and M. K. Chandler, *Managing Large Systems: Organizations for the Future* (New Brunswick, NJ: Transaction Publications, 1971).

A. J. Shenhar and D. Dvir, *Reinventing Project Management: The Diamond Approach to Successful Growth and Innovation* (Boston: Harvard Business School Press, 2007).

F. Siebdrat, M. Hoegel, and H. Ernst, 'How to manage virtual teams', *MIT Sloan Management Review*, Summer (2009), 63–8.

A. L. Stinchcombe and C. Heimer, *Organizational Theory and Project Management: Administering Uncertainty in Norwegian Offshore Oil* (Oslo: Norwegian University Press, 1985).

J. D. Thompson, *Organizations in Action: Social Science Bases of Administrative Theory* (New York: McGraw-Hill, 1967).

J. Woodward, *Industrial Organization: Theory and Practice* (Oxford: Oxford University Press, 1965).

W. Wu, A. Davies, and L. Frederiksen, 'The birth of an eco-city business: Arup's Dongtan project', in G. Grabher and J. Thiel (eds), *Self-Induced Shocks: Mega-Projects and Urban Development* (Berlin: Jovis Verlag GmbH, 2015), 201–20.

Chapter 5: Lean, heavy, and disruptive projects

C. M. Christensen, *The Innovator's Dilemma: When New Technologies Cause Great Firms to Fail* (Boston: Harvard Business School Press, 1997).

K. B. Clark and T. Fujimoto, *Product Development Performance: Strategy, Organization, and Management in the World Auto Industry* (Cambridge, Mass.: Harvard Business School, 1991).

W. Isaacson, *Steve Jobs* (St Ives: Little Brown, 2011).

R. M. Kanter, *When Elephants Learn to Dance: Mastering the Challenges of Strategy, Management, and Careers in the 1990s* (London: Unwin Paperbacks, 1990).

B. Lindsey, *Digital Gehry: Material Resistance/Digital Construction* (Basel: Birkhäuser, 2001).

C. A. O'Reilly and M. T. Tushman, 'The ambidextrous organization', *Harvard Business Review*, April (2004), 74–833.

K. Sabbagh, *21st Century Jet: The Making of the Boeing 777* (London: Pan Books, 1995).

P. Serrador and J. K. Pinto, 'Does agile work? A quantitative analysis of agile project success', *International Journal of Project Management*, 33 (2015), 1040–51.

H. Takeuchi and I. Nonaka, 'The new new product development game', *Harvard Business Review*, January–February (1986), 137–46.

A. Vance, *Elon Musk: How the Billionaire CEO of SpaceX and Tesla is Shaping our Future* (London: Virgin Books, 2015).

S. C. Wheelwright and K. B. Clark, *Revolutionizing Product Development: Quantum Leaps in Speed, Efficiency, and Quality* (New York: The Free Press, 1992).

J. Whyte and R. Levitt, 'Information management and the management of projects', in P. Morris, J. Pinto, and J. S. Söderlund (eds), *The Oxford Handbook of Project Management* (Oxford: Oxford University Press, 2011), 365–88.

J. P. Womack, D. T. Jones, and D. Roos, *The Machine that Changed the World* (New York: MacMillan Publishing Company, 1990).

Chapter 6: London's megaproject ecology

K. Artto, A. Davies, J. Kujala, and A. Prencipe, 'The project business: analytical framework and research opportunities', in P. W. G. Morris, J. Pinto, and J. Söderlund (eds), *The Oxford Handbook of Project Management* (Oxford: Oxford University Press, 2011), 133–53.

B. A. Bechky, 'Gaffers, gofers, and grips: role-based coordination in temporary organizations', *Organization Science*, 17(1) (2006), 3–21.

T. Brady and A. Davies, 'Building project capabilities: from exploratory to exploitative learning', *Organization Studies*, 25(9) (2004), 1601–21.

E. Cacciatori, 'Memory objects in project environments: storing, retrieving and adapting learning in project-based firms', *Research Policy*, 37 (2008), 1591–601.

C. Cattani, S. Ferriani, L. Frederiksen, and F. Täube, 'Project-based organizing and strategic management: a long-term research agenda on temporary organizational forms', *Advances in Strategic Management*, 28 (2011), 3–26.

A. Davies and T. Brady, 'Organisational capabilities and learning in complex product systems: towards repeatable solutions', *Research Policy*, 29 (2000), 931–53.

A. Davies and M. Hobday, *The Business of Projects: Managing Innovation in Complex Products and Systems* (Cambridge: Cambridge University Press, 2005).

A. Davies and I. Mackenzie, 'Project complexity and systems integration: constructing the London 2012 Olympics and Paralympics Games', *International Journal of Project Management*, 32 (2014), 773–90.

A. Davies, D. M. Gann, and T. Douglas, 'Innovation in megaprojects: systems integration at London Heathrow Terminal 5', *California Management Review*, 51(2) (2009), 101–25.

A. Davies, S. MacAulay, T. DeBarro, and M. Thurston, 'Making innovation happen in a megaproject: London's Crossrail suburban railway system', *Project Management Journal*, 45(6) (2014), 25–37.

R. J. DeFillippi and M. B. Arthur, 'Paradox in project-based enterprise: the case of film making', *California Management Review*, 40(2) (1998), 125–39.

M. Dodgson, D. Gann, S. MacAulay, and A. Davies, 'Innovation strategy in new transportation systems: the case of Crossrail', *Transportation Research Part A: Policy and Practice*, 77 (2015), 261–75.

M. Engwall, 'No project is an island: linking projects to history and context', *Research Policy*, 32 (2003), 789–808.

D. Gann, A. Salter, M. Dodgson, and N. Phillips, 'Inside the world of the project baron', *MIT Sloan Management Review*, Spring (2012), 63–71.

D. Gann and A. Salter, 'Innovation in project-based, service-enhanced firms: the construction of complex products and systems', *Research Policy*, 29 (2000), 955–72.

N. Gil, 'Developing cooperative project–client relationships: how much to expect from relational contracts', *California Management Review*, 51(2) (2009), 144–69.

G. Grabher, 'Ecologies of creativity: the Village, the Group and the heterarchic organisation of the British advertising industry', *Environment and Planning A*, 33 (2001), 351–74.

G. Grabher and J. Thiel, 'Projects, people, professions: trajectories of learning through a mega-event (the London 2012 case)', *Geoforum*, 65 (2015), 328–37.

M. Hobday, 'The project-based organisation: an ideal form for management of complex products and systems', *Research Policy*, 29 (2000), 871–93.

R. A. Lundin and A. Söderholm, 'A theory of the temporary organization', *Scandinavian Journal of Management*, 11(4) (1995), 437–55.

R. A. Lundin, N. Arvidsson, T. Brady, E. Ekstedt, C. Midler, and J. Sydow, *Managing and Working in Project Society: Institutional Challenges of Temporary Organizations* (Cambridge: Cambridge University Press, 2015).

S. Manning and J. Sydow, 'Projects, paths and practices: sustaining and leveraging project-based relationships', *Industrial and Corporate Change*, 20(5) (2011), 1369–402.

C. Midler, '"Projectification" of the firm: the Renault case', *Scandinavian Journal of Management*, 11(4) (1995), 363–75.

P. Morris, J. Pinto, and J. S. Söderlund, *The Oxford Handbook of Project Management* (Oxford: Oxford University Press, 2011).

A. Prencipe and F. Tell, 'Inter-project learning: processes and outcomes of knowledge codification in project-based firms', *Research Policy*, 30 (2001), 1373–94.

A. Schwab and A. S. Miner, 'Learning in hybrid-project systems: the effects of project performance on repeated collaboration', *Academy of Management Journal*, 51(6) (2008), 1117–49.

W. R. Scott, R. E. Levitt, and R. J. Orr, *Global Projects: Institutional and Political Challenges* (Cambridge: Cambridge University Press, 2011).

J. Söderlund and F. Tell, 'The P-form organization and the dynamics of project competence: project epochs in Asea/ABB, 1950–2000', *International Journal of Project Management*, 27 (2009), 101–12.

J. Sydow, L. Lindkvist, and R. DeFillippi, 'Project-based organizations, embeddedness and repositories of knowledge: editorial', *Organization Studies*, 25(9) (2004), 1475–89.

A. H. Van Marrewijk, S. Ybema, K. Smits, S. Clegg, and T. S. Pitsis, 'Clash of the titans: temporal organizing and collaborative dynamics in the Panama Canal megaproject', *Organization Studies*, 37(12) (2016), 1745–69.

R. Whitley, 'Project-based firms: new organizational form or variations on a theme?', *Industrial and Corporate Change*, 15(1) (2006), 77–99.

G. Winch, 'Three domains of project organizing', *International Journal of Project Management*, 32 (2014), 721–31.

Chapter 7: Back to the future

T. P. Hughes, *Rescuing Prometheus* (New York: Pantheon Books, 1998).

T. P. Hughes, *Human-Built World: How to Think About Technology and Culture* (Chicago: The University of Chicago Press, 2004).

R. E. Levitt, 'Towards Project Management 2.0', *Engineering Project Organization Journal*, September (2011), 197–210.

McKinsey & Company, 'Infrastructure productivity: how to save $1 trillion a year', The McKinsey Global Institute, The McKinsey Infrastructure Practice, January (2013).

H. W. J. Rittel and M. M. Weber, 'Dilemmas in a general theory of planning'. *Policy Sciences*, 4 (1973), 155–69.

Resources

Systems-based project management textbook:

D. I. Cleland and W. R. King, *Systems Analysis and Project Management* (New York: McGraw-Hill, 1968).

Practitioner guide:

Project Management Institute, *A Guide to the Project Management Body of Knowledge (PMBOK® Guide) 5th Edition* (Newton Square, Pa.: Project Management Institute, 2013).

Recent project management textbooks:

H. Maylor, *Project Management* (Harlow: Prentice Hall, Financial Times, 2005).

J. K. Pinto, *Project Management: Achieving Competitive Advantage* (Boston: Pearson, 2010).

Project management and strategy:

M. Morgan, R. E. Levitt, and W. Malek, *Executing your Strategy: How to Break it Down and Get it Done* (Boston: Harvard Business School Press, 2007).

Megaproject management:

B. Flyvbjerg (ed.), *The Oxford Handbook of Megaproject Management* (Oxford: Oxford University Press, 2017).

E. W. Merrow, *Industrial Megaprojects: Concepts, Strategies, and Practices for Success* (Hoboken, NJ: John Wiley & Sons, 2011).

Case study of the Sydney Opera House:

http://theoperahouseproject.com

Index

A

adaptive project 7, 18, 61, 69, 78,
    86, 90, 106, 127, 130, 132
adhocracy 9, 70–2, 111
administrative adhocracy 71–2
AECOM 134
agile project management 101–2,
    132
airline customers 77, 96–7, 131
Allen, Thomas J. 70
alliance and partnership
    projects 92
Alstom Transport 9
ambidexterity 96
Apollo Programme 54–7, 60, 72
    Boeing Company 56
    contractors 54
    cost of Moon landing 54
    contracts 56
    incentive contracts 56
    Kennedy, John F. 54
    matrix organization 55
    Mueller, George 55
    NASA Program Development
      Plan 55
    Phillips, Samuel C. 55
    systems integration 54
    see also Webb, James E.

Apple 7, 130
    digital hub 7, 91–2
    iTunes 7
    Jobs, Steve 91–2
    portfolio 7
ARPANET 61
array (system of systems) project
    79–80
Arup 62–6, 116, 132, 133
    Arup, Ove 11, 62
    Beijing 2008 Olympics Water
      Cube 74
    Blair, Tony 65
    computer aided design 62
    Integrated Resource Model 66
    Jintao, Hu 65
    matrix organization 65
    Sydney Opera House 62, 66
    Total Design philosophy 62
    see also Dongtan eco-city project
assembly project 79
Association for Project
    Management (APM) 57
Athens Olympic Games 2004 17
Atlas project 13, 39, 44–54, 55, 57,
    60, 61
    AVCO manufacturing
      Corporation 50
    Change Control Board 51

Atlas project (*cont.*)
Consolidated Vultee Aircraft Corporation (Convair) 47, 51, 52
contractors 47–50
digital computer 50
Eisenhower, Dwight D. 45
Glenn L. Martin Company 47, 52
matrix organization 51–2
Minuteman 45, 55
prime contractor 46
project officer 47, 49, 50
project manager 47, 50
Ramo-Wooldridge 45–50, 55
special project office 45
systems engineering 46–9
systems integrator 46–51
Teapot Committee 45, 46
Titan 45, 47, 49
Western Development Division 45, 46, 48
Wooldridge, Dean 45
see also Ramo, Simon; Schreiver, Bernard
atomic bomb 13, 40
autonomy versus integration dilemma 109
autonomous team structure 95–6, 105

B

BAA (formerly British Airports Authority) 104, 109, 119, 122, 131
baseline plan 58
Bechtel 103–4, 114, 116
Bennis, Warren 67
Bernstein, Peter 19
blitz project 82
BMW 15
Boeing 56, 92
Boeing 767 92
Boeing 777 project 14, 86–9, 95, 131
Conduit, Phil 87

Gang of Eight airlines 97
Mulally, Alan 87, 95
Working Together 87, 89
bootlegging projects 93
Boston Big Dig 35, 129
Boston Central Artery/Tunnel 35–7, 60, 129
Brassey, Thomas 11
breakthrough project 91, 92, 93, 97–9
autonomy 98–9
car industry 99–101
Brunel, Isambard Kingdom 10
Brusoni, Stefano 80
bureaucracy 10, 12, 14, 130
budget 58
Burns, T. 67

C

Capital Hospitals 16
car industry 83–6, 99–101
Castells, Manuel 14
CH2M 113, 114, 121
Challenger disaster 59
Champion 19, 34, 84
Chandler, Margaret K. 60
Change Control Board 51
Chilean mine disaster 82
Christensen, Clayton 100, 101
chronological time 81
cities 60, 129
civil engineering 10, 19, 20, 33, 38
Clark, Kim 83, 91, 94, 95
client 11, 63, 65, 113–14, 119–20, 121, 123, 125
climate change 128–30
Clinton, De Witt 22–3, 25, 26, 31, 34
closed system 60, 129
Coca-Cola 15
Cold War 39, 60
collaboration 6, 28, 71, 74, 85, 87, 105, 119, 120

co-location 47, 65, 70, 74–5, 94–5, 121, 133–4
Columbia accident 59
complexity 79–81
compression strategy 72–3
concurrency 50
concurrent development 39, 50, 68–9, 81, 132
configuration management 51
context 18, 108–9
contingency plans 54, 56, 58, 76, 78
contingency theory 67, 75, 82
contract variation 28
contractor 12, 20, 27, 41, 47–50, 103, 105, 115, 119, 120, 124, 125
contracts 3, 27–9, 56–7, 76, 78–9, 103, 105–6, 119–20
cooperation 69, 119–20, 132
    Alliancing 120
    Integrated Program Team 120
coordination 6, 50, 68–9, 73
    see also interdependency
cost 3–4, 35–7, 55, 58, 104–5
creativity 6, 37, 132
cross–functional team 69, 71, 94
Crossrail project 106, 107, 114, 124
    client delivery organization 120
    contracts 120
Crossrail innovation programme 125–6
Crossrail Limited 114

D

Datamaster project 98
Defoe, Daniel 2
DeMeyer, Arnoud 82
derivative project 91, 96–7
design 10, 86–90
    design freeze 50, 101
    preliminary 49
    progressive design freeze 51
    design specification 50, 69
design–build team 87
Digital Project software 134

digital technology 9, 14, 74–5, 86–90, 133–4
    augmented reality 134
    computer-aided design (CAD) 86, 88
    computer-aided manufacture (CAM) 86, 88
    Computer-Aided Three Dimensional Interactive Application (CATIA) 88, 89
    coordination of interdependent tasks 90
    digital communication 94–5
    digital computer 50
    digital information 14, 87
    digital model 90
dispersed team 74–5
disruptive technology 100, 101
doing versus learning dilemma 109–10
Dongtan eco-city project 63–6, 71, 76, 117, 132
Dvir, Dov 17, 77, 81–2

E

eco-city project 63–6
ecological environment 60
eco-technological projects 130
Edmondson, Amy 73–4
Egan, Sir John 104, 117
Eisenhardt, Kathleen 72
electric car 100–1
engineering 10, 37
Engwall, Matts 109
environment 18
    balance stability and innovation 56
    fast-changing 7, 13, 15, 56, 81–2, 117
    predictable 7–8, 56, 117
    stable 7, 12, 56
    turbulent 7
epistemic community 123, 125
Ericsson 3, 81

Erie Canal 19–33
  Big Ditch 23
  budget 25
  Canal Bill 24
  Canal Commissioners 23, 24–5,
    27, 31
  Canal Fund 25
  Canal Law 25
  cement 30–1
  Commissioners' 1817 report 25–6
  competitive tendering 27
  construction 24, 25–30
  contractors 27–9
  cost 23, 24–5, 32
  Deep Cut 29–30
  design 25–7
  Dibble Crane 29, 30
  Erie School of Engineering 32–3
  federal funding 24
  finance 21, 25
  Geddes, James 22, 25, 26, 33
  innovation 29–30
  opening 31–3
  Roberts, Nathan 26, 27, 33
  route 24, 25–6
  survey 22, 26
  Wedding of the Waters 31
  Western Inland Lock Navigation
    Company 21, 23, 24
  White, Canvass 26, 30–1, 32–3
  Wright, Benjamin 23, 25, 26, 33
  see also Clinton, De Witt
event-based time 81
experiential strategy 73

F

fast-competitive project 81
fast-paced conditions 65, 73, 81–2
fixed-capital formation 16
fixed-price contract 7, 56, 103–4
flexible contract 56, 105
flexible project 5, 7, 13–14, 15,
    55–6, 61, 73–4, 78, 86, 98, 102,
    106, 127, 132

flexible team 73–4, 132
Flyvbjerg, Bent 16, 34, 35, 36
Ford, Henry 12
foreseen uncertainty 56, 76
forecasts 35, 59
fountain model 81
fourth constraint 4
framework agreements 122
front end 33–4, 36–7, 131
Fujimoto, Takahiro 83, 95
functional organization 43, 52, 68,
    84, 94, 116
functional team structure 94
funding 20, 21, 24–5, 58

G

Galbraith, Jay 69–70
Gann, David 116
Gehry, Frank 11, 89–90,
    130, 134
global projects 120–1
Google 94
government 9, 15, 130
  approval 23, 46
  funding 22, 23
  politicians 20, 23
  publicly funded projects 60
Grabher, Gernot 122
Great Fire of London 10
Gropius, Walter 62
Groves, Leslie 41, 42, 44, 47
Guggenheim Museum in
    Bilbao 89–90, 130

H

Hall, Peter 5
Hawley, Jesse 21–2
Heatherwick, Thomas 11
heavyweight project manager 85,
    94–5
heavyweight team structure 94–5,
    105
Heimer, Carol 75

Hiding Hand principle 37
High-Speed 1 project 113
Hirschman, Albert O. 37
Hough, George H. 17
Hughes, Thomas P. 13, 60-1, 129

I

IBM Personal Computer 98-9
incentive contract 56, 106
Independent film production
    112-13
industrial revolution 10, 12
infrastructure 12, 20, 129, 133
Infrastructure Industry Innovation
    Platform 125
innovation 6, 7, 11, 14, 15, 29-30,
    37-8, 56, 61, 62, 75, 90-2,
    97-8, 99, 132
innovation balancing act 96-9
innovation in complex projects
    56, 61
innovation projects 90-2
Institution of Civil Engineers 10
integration:
    integration mechanisms 69, 99
    liaison position 69
    linking pins 69
    matrix 69-70
intellectual property 30
intercontinental ballistic missile
    (ICBM) 13, 39, 44-54, 57
interdependency 68-9, 73
International Project Management
    Association (IPMA) 57
International Space Station 1, 58
invitation to tender 3
iron triangle 3
Iridium project 7, 102

J

Jones, Dan 84
Jubilee Line Extension
    project 103-4, 132

K

Kanter, Rosabeth Moss 96, 98
Kodak, Eastman 97

L

Laing O'Rourke (LOR) 113, 117-18,
    124
Lawrence, Paul 69
lean development 83, 85-6
learning 17, 18, 25, 32, 78, 98,
    109-10, 122
Lenfle, Sylvain 61, 78
Lessard, Donald R. 35
lightweight team structure 94, 102
Lindkvist, Lars 81
Loch, Christoph 61, 78, 82
Lockheed Martin 96
London Heathrow Airport
    Heathrow Express project 105
    Terminal 2 project 8-9
    Terminal 5 project (T5) 8, 72,
    104-6, 109, 118, 119, 131
    T5 Agreement 105-6
    T5 Delivery Handbook 106
London 2012 Olympic and
    Paralympic Games 4, 78-9,
    129, 131
    CLM Delivery Partner 113,
    119, 125
    Olympic Delivery Authority
    (ODA) 113, 119, 125
    ODA contracts 78-9
London Underground 9, 115
London's megaproject ecology
    124-6
Lorsch, Jay 69
Lundin, Rolf 15-16, 111

M

McNamara, Robert 57, 60
mainstream project 96-7
managing projects 6

Manhattan Project 13, 39, 40–4, 46, 47, 61
  bomb design 43
  budget 40
  Einstein, Albert 40
  Los Alamos Scientific Laboratory 43
  Manhattan Engineering District 41
  Oppenheimer, Robert J. 43, 47
  outcome 44
  parallel development 42, 44
  plutonium production 40, 41–2
  Roosevelt, Franklin D. 40, 41
  uranium production 40, 41, 42
  see also Groves, Leslie
market uncertainty 77, 91, 97
mass production 7, 12, 15, 67, 128
master builder 10, 11, 90
matrix organization 51, 52, 55, 83, 85, 94, 116
mechanistic organization 67, 73, 76
megaproject 16, 34–7, 104, 107, 124, 129, 132
Miller, Roger 35
Mintzberg, Henry 70–2, 114
modularity 80, 133
Morris, Peter 17, 33
Motorola 7, 102
multidisciplinary team 13, 63
multiple approaches 98
Musk, Elon 100–1, 131–2
mutual adjustment 69, 73

N

National Aeronautics and Space Administration (NASA) 54, 55–7, 59, 60, 72
  Phased Program Planning 84
  zone of uncertainty 56, 69
National Health Service (NHS) 16
newstream project 96–7
Nike 15

Nonaka, Ikujiro 84
novelty 7, 77

O

organic-adaptive 67
organic organization 67
organization theory 67–72
open innovation 92
opening projects 8, 31–3
open system 60, 129
operating adhocracy 71
operational readiness 8
operations 7–9, 13, 15, 33
optimism bias 34, 59
organizational breakdown structure (OBS) 58
organizational memory 112
outcomes 8, 130–1
outputs 8

P

pace 81–2
Panama Canal project 121
parallel development 39, 47, 61, 78, 132
performance 17–18, 34–7
permanent adhocracy 71
personal network 123, 125
Peters, Tom 14
Piano, Renzo 62, 80
Pich, Michael 82
plan 5, 6
platform project 91–2, 93, 95, 96–7
Polaris Programme 51–2, 57, 61
pooled interdependency 68
portfolio 7, 93
Posner, Barry Z. 5
Prencipe, Andrea 80
prime contractor 46, 79
Private Finance Initiative (PFI) 9, 16
procurement 15
product development:
  General Motors 84–5

Honda 85
Japanese approach 85–6, 117
lean development 83, 85–6, 95
overlay approach 86
product development funnel 90
Toyota 85
Western approach 84–5
product life cycle 15
product platform 15
Program Evaluation Review
   Technique (PERT) 52–4, 55
programme 7, 119
project baron 116
project capabilities 116–18, 122,
   123, 128
Project Chess 98–9
project definition 2
project goal 3, 5, 6
project-based firm 114
project-based industry 9, 17, 121
project-based organization 9, 111,
   114–18
project delivery model 105,
   106, 124
project ecology 111, 121–6
   core team 123
   cumulative ecology 123
   disruptive ecology 123
   four layers 122–3
project life cycle 3, 35–6, 58
project management 11, 13, 37, 39,
   46, 57–61
Project Management Body of
   Knowledge (PMBok) 57, 58, 66
Project Management Institute
   (PMI) 57–8, 66, 69
project manager 3, 39, 47
project network 14, 111, 118–21
project nomad 124–5
project organization 2–3, 13, 46,
   52, 79
project phases 3, 33
project proposal 3, 21
Posner, Barry Z. 5
post-industrial society 10, 14, 17

people 134–5
post-industrial organization
   9, 130
post-industrial projects 130–5
psychological safety 74
Public–Private Partnership
   (PPP) 15, 16, 20, 113

R

Raborn, William F. 51
railways 12, 13
Ramo, Simon 45, 47, 50, 59
Randolph, Alan 5
reciprocal interdependency 68–9
regular project 81
Renault 15
repetitive tasks 7–8, 110, 116
Research & Development (R&D)
   projects 70, 92, 97, 98
risk management 6, 58, 76, 77–8
Rogers, Richard 62, 104
Roos, Daniel 84
Royal Institute of British
   Architects 11

S

Sabbagh, Karl 87
Sayles, Leonard R. 60
Scandinavian School of Project
   Studies 108
schedule 6, 50–1, 55
Schreiver, Bernard 45–6, 50, 70
Scott, Richard W. 120–1
Scranton, Philip 12
sequential development 68
sequential interdependency 68
serial development 50
services 8, 9
Shard 80
Shaw, Ronald E. 30
Shenhar, Aaron J. 17, 77, 81–2
shusa 85
side projects 93–4

single-project organization 111,
112–14
skunkwork project 96
smart city 129, 133
Söderlund, Jonas 111
soft opening 8
software development 75
Space Shuttle 58–9
Special Projects Office 45, 51
special purpose vehicle (SPV) 113
specification 2, 7, 10, 26, 28, 49, 84
sponsor 33–4, 99, 131, 132
stable team 73
stakeholders 23, 34, 46, 129, 133
Stalker, G. M. 67
Stinchcombe, Arthur 75
strategic misrepresentation 34
success 4, 8, 34, 130–1
sustaining technology 101
Sydney Opera House 4–5, 62–3, 66
Sydow, Jörg 109
systems approach 13, 51, 60
systems engineering 39, 46, 47–51
systems integrator 46, 133
systems integration 47–51, 54,
80, 119
system project 79
systems project management 55,
60–1
    counter culture and
        opposition 60
    predictable and controlled
        phases 66
    single best way of organizing 66
    standardized and fixed model 66

T

Tabrizi, Behnam 72
Takeuchi, Hirotaka 84
targeted flexibility 78
Taylor, Frederick W. 12
team 3, 5, 6, 10, 72–5
    see also co-location
teaming 74, 102

team structures 94–6
technological gatekeeper 70
technological uncertainty 56, 61,
    / 77, 132
Telford, Thomas 10, 26
temporary adhocracy 71
temporary organization 2, 10, 12,
    14, 67–8, 109
Tesla Motors 100–1
Thames Tideway Tunnel
    Project 125
Thompson, James 68–9
time 6, 50, 81
time-critical project 81–2, 103
time, cost, and quality trade-off 3–4
Toffler, Alvin 9–10, 14, 70, 130, 135
Toshiba 115
transition 8–9
trials 8
trust 70
    shadow of the past 122
    shadow of the future 122
    swift trust 112

U

uncertainty 5, 19, 37, 56, 58, 61, 63,
    73–4, 75–8, 97–9, 102, 127, 132
unforeseen uncertainty 56, 73, 76,
    78, 102
uniqueness 7, 13, 110, 117
unit production 68, 115
urban development 60, 129
    urban problems 60
    urban renewal 60
    see also climate change
urgency 81, 127
    see also pace; time
user requirements 77, 97, 131
Utzon, Jørn 62

V

vanguard project 117–18
virtual team 75

W

waterfall model 68
Waterman, Robert H. 14
Webb, James E. 54, 56
Weber, Max 12
Wheelwright, Steven 91, 94

wicked problems 128–30
Womack, James 84, 99
Woodward, J. 68
Work Breakdown Structure
    (WBS) 33, 58
World Bank 16
Wren, Sir Christopher 10

Index

SOCIAL MEDIA
Very Short Introduction

Join our community
www.oup.com/vsi

- Join us online at the official Very Short Introductions Facebook page.
- Access the thoughts and musings of our authors with our online blog.
- Sign up for our monthly e-newsletter to receive information on all new titles publishing that month.
- Browse the full range of Very Short Introductions online.
- Read extracts from the Introductions for free.
- If you are a teacher or lecturer you can order inspection copies quickly and simply via our website.